2nd Edition

I0123368

DEMOCRACY

HIJACKED

HOW FOREIGN NATIONS ARE USING OUR OWN
POLITICAL SYSTEM AGAINST US

by BJ Williamson

Lanite Publishing, LLC

Dedication

This book is dedicated to our forefathers who risked it all to form an independent nation *"of the people, by the people and for the people"* so that their children and descendants could have a better life. And it is dedicated to those who fought and paid the great price so that we could enjoy freedom from foreign domination and oppression.

God Bless America

Table of Contents

Introduction

When I went in search of the reasons why we lost millions of good jobs to foreign workers, I was surprised when the path led to our own government. And, I was even more surprised to uncover that foreign nations had more clout in our nation's capital than middle class Americans. The only way to restore our country is to find out what is broken and fix it.

Note: Because of the extensive number of sources reference numbers are provided in [brackets] arranged numerically in a list at the back of the book. Certain words have *italics* and <u>underlining</u> added for emphasis in quotations and/or key points. Because it would be burdensome to readers to repeatedly state: "according to" named source, under document heading, by these authors, on this date" each time a source is mentioned you should read with the understanding that information cited is according to the source.

Chapter 1

Tipping the Political Scale

"We the People of the United States, in Order to form a more perfect Union, establish Justice, insure domestic Tranquility, provide for the common defense, promote the general Welfare, and secure the Blessings of Liberty to ourselves and our Posterity, do ordain and establish this Constitution for the United States of America."

Y ou know that powerful political machine that propelled Barack Hussein Obama into power – *Obama didn't build that!* What we are dealing with is much bigger than one politician. Have you noticed that our job losses to foreign workers and trade deficit continue to get worse no matter which party is in power? Just days before our 2012 election, a BBC World Service poll found that 20 out of 21 foreign nations wanted Obama to be US president! [1025] Why?

One reason they want *Obama is because he increased foreign aid 80%!* $20.6 billion of our taxes went to fund foreign business development, foreign militaries, foreign students, and more. [1032]

But our foreign aid pales in comparison to remittances (money transfers) foreign workers in the US send home. Documented remittances *reached $90.7 billion in 2009.* [1037] Hand carried money and *"money sent through financial hubs like London or Dubai are not documented."* [1037] When you add undocumented remittances our real cost is probably *"50% higher!"* [1032] In 2012, remittances increased *"faster than expected."* [1038]

How Foreign Nations Tip Our Political Scale

A Pew Research Center survey in 2010 found *"public confidence in the federal government at one of the lowest points in half-century."* [796] Yet, incumbents keep getting re-elected. How?

Foreign nations have found a way to use our own political system against us. Historically having two major political parties helped balance the needs and priorities of citizens. However, when a scale is in balance it can easily be tipped either way. Our political parties divide our nation roughly 50% Republican and 50% Democrat. We balance each other out. Special interest groups as small as 1% can tip our political scale to get their agenda passed. Politicians who go along with their agenda get money. Politicians who don't are targeted for removal.

The number one goal for foreign nations was access to US computer systems. Why? Our computers were protective storage vaults that: secured strategic military and government data, guarded US high tech product designs, controlled financial transactions for billions of dollars, held personal data on US citizens, and more.

Foreign nations hit the jackpot in 1990 when they got Congress to pass H-1B legislation that let foreign programmers take jobs in the US. The H-1B visas made it easy to raid the vaults. They didn't have to hack our computers-they were given inside access. "Non-immigrant" H-1B visas were used to displace millions of Americans with foreign programmers.

The H-1B impact was so bad that *California, New York, Illinois, and Virginia now have more foreign born information technology (IT) workers than native born IT workers!* [59] Think about this when you use electronic voting machines programmed in the USA.

How did foreign nations get our politicians to turn against US citizens they were sworn to protect?

Money tipped the scales. Overall, the computer/internet political contributions increased 2363%, from 1990 to 2000! [424] It spiked even higher in 2008 and 2012. [1057]

This money flowed to both political parties through PACs, soft money, and individual contributions. In 2000, Dr. Matloff, an outspoken critic of the H-1B visas, who witnessed firsthand the harm caused to American programmers, said it best, *"Congress has been bought off equally... Neither party dares to cross the industry."* [337]

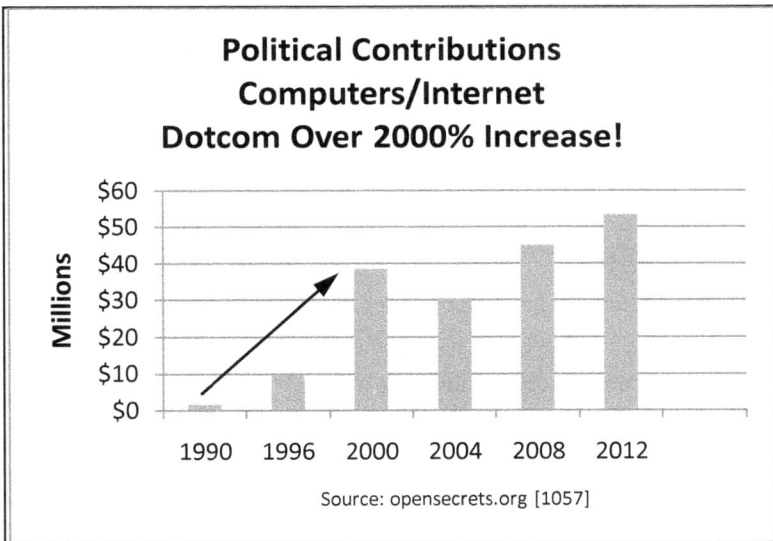

Political Contributions Computers/Internet Dotcom Over 2000% Increase!

Source: opensecrets.org [1057]

Eighty five percent of the jobs H-1Bs take are entry level jobs that should have gone to young Americans graduating from college. Moreover, the H-1B gave foreigners hands-on training in our country that in turn enabled offshoring our professional jobs.

Our Politicians Are Not Representing Us

Our elected politicians are supposed to be public servants. We obviously cannot have all citizens meeting to discuss and debate legislation. That would be unmanageable.

So our government was set up to be run by elected representatives. Their role was to assemble, debate, and pass laws in accordance with the will of the US citizens they represent. As a result we have a few hundred elected representatives passing laws that impact 300 million Americans. They tax us and spend our tax dollars.

In violation of our public trust, many of our politicians stopped representing us. For example, in October 2000, despite Americans' strong opposition to increasing H-1B visas for foreign workers, Congress passed the increases anyway. US Rep. Tom Davis (R-VA) and Chair of the Republican Congressional Campaign explained why: *"This is not a popular bill with the public. It's popular with the CEOs ... This is a very important issue for the high-tech executives who give the money."* [24]

American programmers pleaded with Congress to repeal the H-1B legislation and stop companies from offshoring their jobs. They were in an unfair fight much bigger than they ever imagined. The first surprise punch was discovering Congress would not stop executives from hiring H-1Bs and offshoring, because our own government was also hiring H-1Bs and offshoring. The second blow came when Americans found themselves up against big lobbies bulging with brass knuckle outsourcing money in their gloves.

Hence when the flame of citizens' protests over visa fraud, and foreign governments raiding US jobs flared, they were doused with big money.

Hardworking Americans Blindsided

H-1B visas allowed foreigners to take US jobs that required a college education. Guess where they got their college education–USA. Guess who paid for their college–YOU.

A survey of Americans in high tech jobs in 2001, found that *85% were worried they may lose their job to a non-citizen.* [53] Hardworking college-educated Americans bought homes based on expected future earnings. They were blindsided when they lost their programming, engineering, accounting, and other high paying jobs to foreign workers. Their job losses fed the foreclosure feeding frenzy that spread across the US turning out the lights in Americans' homes across our country.

It was cruel. Americans were forced to default on mortgages for their homes where many had built up several years of equity. Banks and foreigners gobbled up Americans' homes at bargain bankruptcy rates.

By June 2003, home foreclosures in the US reached record levels with almost 1 out of every 100 homes in foreclosure. [143] By 2008, one in 54 homes received a foreclosure filing. [723] In 2009, *"For the first time in U.S. history, banks own a greater share of residential housing net worth in the United States than all individual Americans put together."* ("The Middle Class in America is Radically Shrinking. Here Are the Stats to Prove it.") [860]

"1.9 Million 2011 Foreclosures are Fewest Since 2007," a 2012 AP report said the drop was because of legal delays not improvements. [920] Almost 8 million families lost their homes over this 4 year period! Lost jobs made it impossible to pay mortgages. *Our politicians and media so quick to elicit empathy for the children of illegal aliens, showed no empathy for the millions of young innocent American children devastated by the loss of their homes.* [1039]

Millionaires in Congress

While middle class Americans lost jobs, insurance, and homes, the number of US millionaires grew.

In 2009, the number of millionaires jumped 16% to 7.8 million. Just 1% of the people owned 83% of US stocks. [860] What's surprising is who some of these millionaires are.

Our unemployment hit 10.2 percent. At the same time 44 percent of our Congress members were millionaires, according to Politico's: "Report: 237 Millionaires in Congress." For example, it estimated Secretary of State Hillary Clinton had $21 million and Barack Obama had $4 million. The article cited a Center for Responsive Politics study that found not only were members of Congress drawing six figure salaries, *many were invested in companies that received taxpayer financed bailouts such as "Wells Fargo, Citigroup, Goldman Sachs and Bank of America."* [802]

Of course, we need politicians who are skilled money managers. If a business owner became a millionaire running an honest business that created jobs for Americans and generated wealth in our economy, they could be a great political leader.

However, it is another matter if some members of Congress became millionaires by exploiting their public servant roles. It is not acceptable if their millions came from insider trading tips or favored investor positions for IPOs. It is not okay if they passed laws that benefited companies they invested in, or that offered them jobs.

How many members of Congress own stocks in US companies that gave them political contributions to pass H-1B and/or offshore tax incentives legislation? Something is wrong. If they were brilliant money managers, the US economy would not be in a financial crisis.

China's Influence Buying

Millions of dollars were channeled to both political parties to advance trade and aid to Communist China during our elections.

According to a report, "Red Tide: The Chinese Communist Targeting America" by The McAlvany Intelligence Advisor, our job losses to China trace back to when *Richard Nixon and Henry Kissinger* opened the flood gates for outsourcing US manufacturing jobs to China in 1972. They pitted American workers against millions of slave laborers and workers paid less than a dollar an hour in China. [173]

The FBI issued warnings in 1991 when they discovered China channeled money through intermediaries to manipulate our elections. This foreign tampering may have been going on undetected for years. In what McAlvany called the "biggest political scandal in U.S. history" evidence was uncovered that, *"Red China bought favorable trade policy by pouring millions of dollars into the re-election of Bill Clinton."* The National Security Agency intercepted communications that 30 US Congressional candidates were targeted for influence buying. [173]

Take a moment and think about what kind of US candidates China would select. They want people they can control. Think about what China expected in return for the money.

The report claimed that *both Democrat and Republican politicians received "contributions" in the form of, "payoffs, commissions, finder's fees, kickbacks, or outright bribes from the Chinese Communist government and from U.S. multinational corporations wishing to do business in China."* [173] This is key to understanding why Congress does not represent us.

India's Strategy to Influence US Elections

If you are concerned about the millions of professional jobs lost to foreign workers, you may be surprised to learn that India took almost 50 out of every one hundred US citizens' jobs lost to H-1B visa workers. No other country came close. China was in second place taking approximately 9 out of every 100 US citizens' jobs lost to H-1Bs.

H-1Bs paved the way for offshoring our programming jobs, accounting jobs, and other jobs done on computers. India took more of these 'knowledge" jobs than any other foreign country. For example, in 2002, *India took 85 out of every 100 US computer information technology (IT) jobs that were offshored.*

"The American political process at one level is transparent and simple – you pay money, you get results," was a disturbing proclamation written in a 2002, article, "USINPAC – Indian Toehold in US Political Whirlpool" published by the *Indian Express* in Mumbai, India. [521]

Laid off Americans had no money to buy political influence. However, people making money off visa workers and offshoring had a lot of money. And pay money they did. Indian-Americans "donated" over $7 million to the 2000 US presidential election. The money was given to both Democrats and Republicans. In return, the US India Political Action Committee (USINPAC) expected regular monthly breakfast meetings with key US senators, and lunch with US congressional aides *"who pull the strings and write policy documents."* [521]

What results did USINPAC want? It wanted to increase immigration from India, to increase US aid to India, to increase jobs offshored to India, and to expand political power in the US for people from India. [521]

Not For Sale At Any Price

There are several red flags that our government has gone off course. Why would our government not want to verify voters were US citizens qualified to vote? Why did our government tax us to subsidize millions of foreign students; and then pass H-1B visa worker legislation that let them take our jobs? These questions and more will be explored. [59]

Recall the H-1B is a *temporary "non-immigrant"* visa. Yet, most stay illegally when their visas expire. They want amnesty.

Displaced American workers protested to no avail since the H-1B visa legislation was passed in 1990. [289]

In 2000 this temporary program turned 10 years old, and continued even though *the US Department of Commerce found no proof that a shortage of American programmers existed, and was alarmed that 28% of new programming jobs were going to H-1Bs*. [26] This was a foreign takeover of the IT industry Americans created.

Now this "temporary" visa program is 23 years old!

Our future and our children's' future is at stake. We must stop foreign tampering with our elections. The good news is that united we are much more powerful than a few corrupt executives and politicians.

Even though it can be risky to speak out, it is more risky to remain silent while our country is headed for an economic and national security train wreck. If you are a US citizen you are on board. Whether we like it or not our government has been hijacked, and we are the only ones who can take it back.

If you don't know the history, you're doomed to make the same mistakes again and again. (Edmund Burke)

Wouldn't you like to know what's been going on in our nation's capital? It is time to pull back the curtain.

Chapter 2

Executives Buy Political

Influence

Then: "Government of the People, by the People, for the People"–Abe Lincoln

Now: Government of the PACs, by the Corporations, for the Executives

Our executives were targeted by foreign nations. For example, The South Asia Analysis Group published a strategy paper by Hari Sud, a graduate of Punjab University and the University of Missouri, on how to protect India's outsourcing interests during our 2004 US Presidential election. [131] Sud advised, *"the trade issue has to be addressed in such a way that a few high paying jobs in America are made dependent on trade with India."* [131]

Imagine all India needed were about 500 CEOs in our top corporations, and about 500 politicians. The trick was to tie multi-million dollar CEO bonuses to outsourcing; and then to use "contributions," insider deals, and the "revolving door" to turn US politicians into multi-millionaires.

The Enron case provided a glimpse into widespread political influence buying. [8] About 71 senators and 188 representatives got political contributions from Enron. [286] If you went to visit Congress that year and shook hands with Senators and Representatives almost every other handshake would be with a hand that got money from Enron.

Accounting Deceptions Made Legal

Executives made political *"contributions"* to get laws passed. One big payoff came in 1995, when the Financial Accounting Standards Board passed rules that did not require companies to expense the cost of stock options. These accounting rules allowed executives to both hide the cost of their stock options, and to overstate profits. [7] As a result, we were subsidizing executives' income, while making investments based on inflated financial statements. [286]

Individual Contributions Soared

Our forefathers carefully structured our government to give citizens fair and equal representation. However, it has become painfully clear that a few wealthy individuals exert undue influence over our politicians. [16] Executives in Silicon Valley California became adept at tipping the scale to get legislation passed that allowed them to take big bonuses. [23]

Individuals can contribute $4,000 to a congressional candidate, and up to $50,000 to a political party per election. Rich people can get around the limits. They can have their family members donate. Looking at the 2000 election as an example, by October, 530 people contributed the maximum allowed. [16] This meant that a small percentage of US citizens, *less than one hundredth of 1%* wielded a lot of power over our political candidates.

From Democracy to PACocracy

Political Action Committees (PACs) became a major source of funding for US political races in the 1950s and grew increasingly powerful. [424] PACs make contributions in the hundreds of millions of dollars. [16] As their wealth went up, ours went down.

Executives and College Leaders form Lobbies

Executives wanted to replace Americans with cheaper visa workers. US university leaders wanted to fill our graduate schools with foreign students to get government research grants. They joined forces to create lobbies. [22] They were like Bonnie & Clyde raiding our government coffers. Executives provided the money to prime the pump. And universities provided the "studies" creating illusions of worker shortages.

When they wanted more taxpayer research money each year executives and academic leaders portrayed themselves as concerned about maintaining our nation's technology leadership. The sincerity of their concern is hard to believe. They are the ones who gave foreign access to our research and laid off the Americans who had made us the world's technology leader.

Several company CEOs are members of multiple lobbies. This appears similar to registering to vote under multiple names. Following are a small sampling of the lobbies.

COUNCIL ON COMPETITIVENESS

The Council on Competitiveness lobbied for US taxpayer funding for industry research. [484]

■ *Business members included: IBM, Lockheed Martin, Cisco, Hewlett Packard (HP), QUALCOMM, Lucent, Xerox...*

■ *Academic members included: MIT, Carnegie Mellon, Harvard, University of California, University of Michigan, University of Texas, Virginia Tech, University of Wisconsin.... [486]*

■ *Partners included: the Assoc. of American Universities, Compete America, Semiconductor Industry Assoc., and The Alliance for Science and Technology Research in America (ASTRA)...*

♦ *The partner memberships overlap, for example, the ASTRA members include: GE, IBM, HP, Lucent, General Motors... [487]*

COMPETE AMERICA—"ANTI-AMERICAN WORKER CARTEL"

When the Senate considered cutting back on H-1B visas, executives formed the *American Business for Legal Immigration* and commissioned university studies to *"support its position."* [24] The lobby later changed its name to Compete America. Its members grew to *"over 200 corporations, universities, research institutions; and trade associations."* [446]

In 2005 Compete America sent a letter to Congress warning that our technology leadership was at risk, and that its members were committed to keeping the US competitive. [450]

However, Communications Workers of America published, "Compete America!–Story of An Anti-American Worker Cartel." [446] that claimed Compete America sent "editorials" to the *Wall Street Journal, BusinessWeek* and *The New York Times* that were used to lobby for H-1B visas. And that Compete America also lobbied *to increase visas for students from China and India, to exempt foreign graduate students from immigration caps, and to speed up granting green cards.* The article warned that Compete America *may be trying to take monopoly control of recruiting by setting up a nationwide employee database to screen US job applicants.* [446]

LOBBIES PROMOTE OFFSHORING TO CHINA

The Asian American Manufacturers Association (AAMA) was founded in 1980 by eight Chinese engineers to persuade US companies to offshore to the Pacific Rim. They sought assistance from our federal, state and local governments. [372]

- *The biggest pro-China lobby, The Business Coalition for U.S.-China Trade, had over 1,000 US corporate members including: "Boeing, Motorola, General Motors, General Electric, United Technologies, Mobil, Exxon, Caterpillar, Cargill, Philip Morris, Proctor and Gamble, TRW, Westinghouse, ..." [173]*

INFORMATION TECHNOLOGY ASSOCIATION OF AMERICA (ITAA)

ITAA is a lobby for *computer manufacturers, defense contractors, electronic voting machine manufacturers, Internet companies, outsourcing companies, plus IT associations in 50 other countries.* [115] ITAA lobbied for H-1B visas, electronic voting machines, and more. [556] ITAA president Harris Miller testified in defense of IT offshoring at a 2003 House Small Business Committee hearing. (Did Congress know that *Miller was also chairman of the World Information Technology and Services Alliance that represented IT groups from 53 countries!*) Congress was alarmed by forecasts that 3.3 million US high tech jobs were at risk of offshoring. Miller said the "bigger picture" was our $7.9 billion IT services trade surplus. [115] We created the IT industry and expect an IT surplus. It is our "oil."

- *ITAA paid Global Insight to do "studies." A 2004 "study" declared offshoring IT services was good for the US economy.* [20] [81] *Another "study" predicted offshoring IT would create 317,387 new US jobs by 2008.* [129]

- *ITAA's 400 corporate members included: IBM, Intel, Microsoft, AT&T, Boeing, Dell, HP, PricewaterhouseCoopers, Lockheed Martin, Northrop Grumman, Oracle, Accenture, Amazon, AOL ...* [556] *According to SourceWatch "registered lobbyists for ITAA's "NET" PAC are identical to those of ITAA itself."* [556]

To consolidate lobbying by US technology companies, ITAA merged with other lobbies in 2008. ITAA Chairman Hank Steininger said, "the technology industry had insufficient clout in Washington and the state capitals-until now." The goal was a "robust grassroots-to-global capability for the technology industry at large." It had an "exclusive membership with the World Information Technology and Services Alliance (WITSA)" based in Beijing and Brussels. Ironically, the consolidated lobby was named the Technology Association of America (TechAmerica). [973] From *grassroots-to-global means moving our technology companies from America, to offshore!*

COMPUTER SYSTEMS POLICY PROJECT

The Computer Systems Policy Project, in Washington, claimed trying to protect US jobs would hamper innovation, stifle economic growth, and result in higher unemployment. Its members were *Intel, IBM, Dell, HP, and more.* [114] [222]

TECHNET LOBBY

John Doerr founded TechNet in 1997 as a bipartisan PAC. *"Dotcom titans"* and other Silicon Valley executives joined TechNet to oppose a California initiative that would make it easier for shareholders to sue companies that mismanaged their money. At the time Doerr, a co-founder of a large venture capital firm, "had a stake in more than 250 technology ventures." [559] Doerr *"helped raise a record $40 million to oppose the shareholder proposition, ensuring its defeat."* [559] [558] Notice that *"Dotcom titans"* were worried about lawsuits 3 years prior to the dotcom crash.

A few more TechNet Political Victories:

■   *Got the US Senate to approve permanent normal trade relations with China in 2000. And got the H-1B visa cap increased to 195,000 per year.* [559] [560] [22] [184]

■   *Got "stimulus package" lobbied for, and then wrote a thank you letter to Bush in 2002. They claimed to be committed to "promoting the long-term growth and strength of the U.S. economy."* [195]

■   *"Maintained favorable accounting treatment for stock options granted to outside directors by defeating the Financial Standards Accounting Board's proposal that these options be expensed."* [558]

TechNet's members were CEOs from the IT industry, biotech industry, venture capital firms, investment banks, and law firms. Its affiliates: *Semiconductor Industry Association, Business Software Alliance, Silicon Valley Manufacturing Group, ITAA....* [558]

FINANCE AND LAW FIRM LOBBIES

Lawyers and law firms dwarfed IT industry contributions. . They gave $180.8 million in 2012. A *NewsMax.com* article, "H-1B: Bombing the Middle Class" said the US has 15,000 immigration lawyers profiting from H-1B visas. [52] Lawyers made millions processing H-1B visas, according to, "Indentured Servants for High-Tech Trade Labor" an article in the Baltimore Sun. [468] The American Immigration Lawyers Association (AILA) website provided clients with a "Take Action" hypertext link to *tell Congress: not to sign the SAVE act that would deport people in the US illegally, to approve more H-1B visas, to pass the DREAM Act, etcetera.* [677]

The Finance/Insurance/Real Estate industry dwarfed the legal industry. They gave $573.6 million in 2012. Interestingly, they gave Romney three times what they gave Obama.

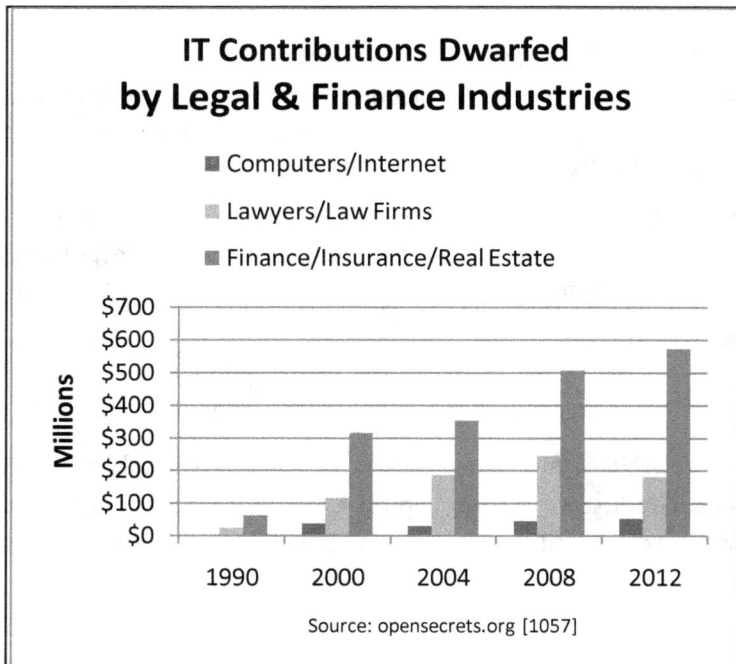

IT Contributions Dwarfed
by Legal & Finance Industries

■ Computers/Internet

▩ Lawyers/Law Firms

■ Finance/Insurance/Real Estate

Source: opensecrets.org [1057]

It is Time to End or Reform CEO Lobbies

This was just a small sampling of lobbies influencing Congress. They interweave and twist and turn making it hard to know where money is coming from and whose agendas they represent.

Industries would not give millions in 'contributions' to our political campaigns unless they expected something in return.

These lobbies create a complicated web encircling and controlling our politicians. They build their web, use their "studies" to lure, pounce like a giant spider, and then suck out our tax dollars faster than we can replenish them.

It is time to clean out the network webs and stop the corruption. We need to end lobbies that do not work for the interests of Americans and America.

Chapter 3

Revolving Door Lures Political

Favors

The doors to our Capital and Tax Dollars Go Round and Round.

One big story not getting the media coverage it deserves is how our government and our military leaders are being lured by corporations. The revolving door entices government officials into abusing their positions to line up lucrative private sector jobs. They pass legislation, spin the revolving door and get rich cashing in on government contracts and contacts. It's better than roulette. Companies recruiting former government officials say they are not doing anything wrong. However, spinning the revolving door turns some $100,000 a year former government officials into multi-millionaires.

"Two ex-senators Join Major Lobbying Firm" was the title of a January 11, 2011 post on *usatoday.com*. The article claimed that Byron Dorgan a Democrat who retired and Robert Bennett a Republican who lost his re-election bid were hired by Arent Fox LLP. This law firm lobbies to influence *"health care, trade, and technology and financial policy."* The article said, *"It is a time-honored tradition for ex-lawmakers to join the ranks of law firms with lobbying shops."* While the law forbids them to lobby Congress directly for one year, they can begin advising clients right away. [881]

Clinton Revolving Door

The revolving door was in full swing at the time of the Enron fiasco. The *Clinton Administration approved over $1 billion in subsidized loans to Enron's overseas projects.* In turn, Democrats got $2 million in contributions according to, "Enron's India Connections Likely to Haunt Clinton." [593] "Crony Capitalism, Clinton-Style," in 1994 reported Clinton's *"Arkansas cronies he'd named to the Export-Import Bank board"* used $3 billion of our taxes to help Enron build a power plant in India, and in turn Enron contributed *"$100,000 to Clinton's dirty-money reelection effort."* [285]

After he left office, Clinton became *Honorary Chairperson for the American India Foundation* along with co-chairs Rajat Gupta (*An outsourcing kingpin as head of McKinsey & Company*) and Victor Menezes. [280] McKinsey hired Chelsea Clinton for $120,000! Reporters *speculated her value came from her parents contacts estimated to be worth 20 times her salary.* [282] [283] Young Americans had trouble finding jobs because of outsourcing and Chelsea gets $120,000!

The *William J. Clinton Foundation*:

- *Brokered an agreement in 2003 that let India drug companies sell cut rate AIDS drugs to South Africa.* [284]

- *Clinton helped launch a Chinese government backed internet search engine company in 2004 that "donated" an undisclosed amount of money to his foundation.* [277]

- *In 2008* Clinton raised $353 million for his foundation, *including money from the Saudi's, the United Arab Emirates, Kuwait, Qatar, and more. Clinton said:* "Every single Palestinian I know in America is a millionaire or a college professor." [840]

- *"Saudi Government, Other Nations Donate Millions to Clinton Foundation," was a 2010 foxnews.com report.* [869]

- *A 2010 AP story asked, "Why was Clinton getting millions of dollars from the Middle East?"*

Revolving Door Recruited to Lobby for China

The revolving door with China has been spinning for a long time. Recall the "Red Tide" report said Henry Kissinger played a key role in opening trade with China. It also *reported that several former US government officials were recruited to lobby for China.* It named Kissinger and Alexander M. Haig, Jr. as leaders of the pro-China lobby. As consultants they advised US corporations on contracts with communist China. [173]

Government Contractors Revolving Door

The top 20 Federal Contractors *hired 224 people who had been Congressional members or government officials* according to a 2004 Project on Government Oversight (pogo) report, "Government Contractors Wield Influence through Revolving Door, Campaign Contributions." [440]

War Millionaires

Some of the most disturbing "revolving door" connections involve military contractors. Franklin Roosevelt and Harry Truman fought against war profiteering. However, an analysis by *United for a Fair Economy* and the *Institute for Policies,* "War Millionaires: Defense Contractor CEO Pay Up 200 Percent Since 9/11," found CEOs *"personally profiting from the horrors of war."* [736]

The Homeland Security Research Corporation forecasted that homeland security spending would increase *from $5 billion in 2000 to $103 billion by 2010.* [441] That's over a 20 fold increase! These billions create financial incentives for CEOs to persuade our government to prolong the war.

It is disturbing that some people, and some foreign nations are getting rich from a war where young Americans are risking their lives, suffering life altering injuries, and many are dying.

Carlyle Group –Revolving Door "Investing in War"

Former president George H. W. Bush, former Secretary of State Jim Baker, former Secretary of defense Frank Carlucci, former head of the FCC William Kennard, and former SEC head Author Levitt were among the former government officials hired by the Carlyle Group according to a 2002, *Fortune* article. It claimed some former officials made millions from Carlyle dealings. [341]

Carlyle has been wary of media attention. It is one of the world's biggest private-equity buyout firms. It bought shares in US defense contractors and US telecom companies. And, *Carlyle invested in Silicon Valley dotcom startups.* [341]

From 1998-2002, The Carlyle Group raised $14 billion! It became the 14th largest Department of Defense contractor. Some investors were Saudis including the bin Laden's. [341] [377]

By 2003, Carlyle was "the ninth largest Pentagon contractor." [441]

"Investing in War: The Carlyle Group profits from government and conflict" was a subtitle in the 2004, The Center for Public Integrity, report, *"Outsourcing the Pentagon."* It claimed Carlyle Group investors had <u>made billions of dollars</u>. [442]

Carlyle was helping companies in India, "scale up and get access to the knowledge and markets they seek," said Shankar Narayanan, head of its operations in India. In 2005 *BusinessWeek* reported, "Private Equity Pours into India," and *that the Carlyle Group had invested $50 million in India from 2003-2005.* [721] Was the Carlyle revolving door providing India access to proprietary US defense industry technology and contracts, and accelerating offshoring of strategic US industries?

Carlyle Clones

Carlyle is not the only one. A Center for Public Integrity article, "The Sincerest Form of Flattery" reported that Carlyle's revolving door model was being copied: "Like Carlyle, Paladin and Arlington Capital Partners have enlisted several former political and military leaders," [441]

It is Time to Stop the Spin

The revolving door appears to lubricate the skids for shipping American wealth overseas.

It is self destructive to have politicians pass legislation that causes US taxpayers, the major source of support for our government, to lose their jobs.

Regulations on former government officials, especially former presidents, with regard to foreign companies, foreign investing, government contracts, and foreign governments need to be carefully considered and addressed. The revolving door endangers our national security. It is time to stop the spin.

Chapter 4

"Stimulus Packages" that

Harm America

This trail is not just crumbs, it is big money.

Follow the money trails to uncover how "stimulus packages" were like a bank heist. Foreign "gangsters" made off with bags of money we borrowed, and then we were sent the bill to pay for it. A few examples of "stimulus" money gone wrong:

Bailout Money Channeled to Foreign Countries!

"Will GM Spend Taxpayer Bailout Money on Overseas Operations?" a 2009 report exposed: "*U.S. Operations Received $50 Billion in Taxpayer Funds—And Now May Send Millions of Dollars Overseas.*" GM wanted to spend US economic stimulus money in China and Europe! Dan Ikenson of the Cato Institute insisted that executives knew best how to make a profit and that, "*We should not infringe on their decision-making.*" [794] If these executives knew how to make profits, they would not need a bailout. They created the US economic crisis by offshoring; and then, they wanted our government to infringe on us to pay the cost of their poor management decisions.

In 2013 we may lose 50% of what we paid for GM stock in a buyback! One critic said "*One hopes all those Union votes were well worth the now booked $40+ billion cost to all taxpayers.*" [1040]

Stimulus For Who?

Obama's stimulus bill was projected to cost $862 billion. In comparison, a *Fox News* 2010 article, "CBO: Eight Years of Iraq War Cost Less Than Stimulus Act," showed costs for eight years of war in Iraq totaled $709 billion. [868]

And, what did the Obama Team do with stimulus money borrowed from China? Well, Obama's Energy Secretary Steven Chu channeled some of the economic recovery money to fund building wind turbines in China. Senator Chuck Schumer asked Chu not to approve federal funding for this project. Chu tried to justify his actions by claiming it put Americans to work installing the turbines. [858] So, we borrowed money from China, used it to stimulate China's economy, and then we are supposed to reimburse China?

But that is not all; even Democrats were appalled at how Obama's team was distributing stimulus money. A *Fox News* report, "Dem Lawmakers to Call for Suspension of Stimulus Going to Foreign Firms," said senators Chuck Schumer, Sherrod Brown, Robert Casey and Jon Tester asked for a freeze on the Recovery Act program after they discovered *"a majority of the program's grants went to foreign-owned companies."* [858] This is outrageous, no US economic stimulus money should have gone to foreign companies. American taxpayers have a right to know which foreign companies got stimulus money. These companies should be required to pay back all the money including interest, and other costs incurred.

Our economic crisis was created by offshoring, yet Obama's team was channeling US stimulus money to foreign companies. Either Obama's team was incompetent, or worse they were intentionally trying to cause an US economic collapse.

Economic Stimulus Money Fueled the War?

We want to end our dependence on foreign oil. Yet, Congress repeatedly passed "economic stimulus" legislation that increased US demand for foreign oil, and created a windfall for Arab nations.

The Clinton Administration's 1996 *"economic stimulus,"* allowed small businesses to take a tax write-off for the purchase of 6,000 pound SUVs. [571] These tax incentives were so skewed that consultants, salespersons, real estate agents, and others, who did not need large vehicles, could buy a $50,000 SUV and take a 100% tax write off. In other words, if they bought a gas guzzler the vehicle was free. For every 100,000 SUVs deducted, it cost us about $5 billion in tax write offs. [417] No doubt several hundred thousand SUV's were written off. [418]

Not to be outdone, the *"Hummer tax break"* passed by the Bush Administration *"virtually made all three-ton, business-use SUVs fully deductible in the first year."* This 2003 Jobs and Growth Act raised the tax deduction from $25,000 to $100,000 per vehicle! [675]

Even though in 2004 Congress cut the tax deduction back to $25,000, critics claimed that this legislation was *fueling the war*, and that poor Americans were subsidizing the rich. The 50% bonus deduction combined with the $25,000 depreciation expense still let businesses write off the full expense of $50,000 SUVs. [675]

Worst of all, *every time a small business owner bought a SUV that got 12 mpg instead of a more efficient vehicle that got 24 mpg this doubled the amount of fuel they had to purchase.* Small business owners do a lot of driving. This "stimulus" skyrocketed US demand for gas and harmed our economy.

Bailouts of Mismanaged Multinational Banks

US banks converted to multinational banks, yet when they got in financial trouble they claimed to be American banks. It's like having your sweetheart take your money and cheat with someone else, and when the money runs out they have the audacity to ask you for more money. We treated our banks well. We deposited our money and made payments on time. Then our banks took our money and cheated on us secretly making risky overseas loans.

"Panel: Gov't Bailout of AIG Was 'Poisonous,'" a 2010 *Fox News* report said the bailout *"distorted the marketplace by transforming highly risky... bets into fully guaranteed payment obligations."* They gambled and we paid for it.

The justification for the bailout was to *"prevent a collapse of big financial institutions and to repay their trading partners."* [859] These were payments to "raiding partners" to not "trading partners." We should not be taxed to repay foreign investors who caused the financial crisis and got rich from offshoring. When US banks shifted money offshore they caused US job losses which in turn caused people to default on mortgages. American homes were not "toxic assets," the toxic assets were offshore financial siphons draining the life out of our economy.

Stimulus Money Role in the Economic Crisis

These stimulus packages were more a result of crafty lobbying than an effort to restore our economy. It should not be legal to tax us to guarantee multinational banks, nor to bail out foreign investors, nor to encourage buying gas guzzlers. This does not stimulate our economy, it tears down our economy.

Chapter 5

Lobbies for Foreign Countries!

Guess Who's Driving The Train?

W e are heading for an economic train wreck. You will be surprised who is driving our political policies. Congress members, who are supposed to be driving our economic train into prosperity, are selling tickets to the highest bidders from foreign countries and letting them take a turn at the wheel.

Foreign governments lobby our Congress. And, many immigrants granted US citizenship formed ethnic lobbies to benefit their ethnic group and country of origin. Also, some foreign workers in the US on visas or illegally, who complained that they were taxpayers with no political power, underhandedly exerted political influence *"by making careful donations to key movers and shakers in the US Congress."* [30]

Because India dominates both the H-1Bs and offshoring of US professional jobs, we will look at lobbies with connections to India. As you read keep in mind that you would not want to be judged by the actions of a few greedy US executives who harmed Americans and treated foreign workers like indentured servants. Nor should we judge most people living in India because a few greedy people who emigrated from India not to become Americans and meld with the American people, but rather to get rich by exploiting our country and our people.

US India Political Action Committee (USINPAC)

Immigrants from India "*launched their very first professional clearing house for money—the US-India Political Action committee or USINPAC.*" Recall the "USINPAC – Indian Toehold in US Political Whirlpool," claimed: "*The American political process at one level is transparent and simple—you pay money, you get results.*" [521] The "results" they wanted were government posts that set "*US cyber policy*" and "media visible" posts like the US Surgeon General. [521]

Indian companies took US politicians on "*lavish junkets to India in an effort to influence US legislation,*" according to "The Social Contract" essay Rob Sanchez wrote about USINPAC. He said that in return politicians agreed to increase H-1B quotas and not restrict offshoring. Sanchez asked if these politicians violated "*due process by making covert agreements with foreign nations.*" [414]

To gain US political clout USINPAC's executive director Sanjay Puri "*lured two senior officers from pro-Israeli PACs*" who taught him to use money as a carrot, "*any mis-step and the money dries up.*" The plan was "*organize, participate, donate and demand.*" [521] USINPAC dangled carrots and our politicians like donkeys pulled their plow through Congress as they planted visa and offshoring legislation.

USINPAC covered all the bases. They gave money to federal, state, and local campaigns of Democrats and Republicans. The US India House Caucus, the biggest caucus lobbying the House, was co-chaired by Rep. Joe Crowley (D-NY), and Rep. Joe Wilson (R-SC). USINPAC's Senate caucus originally recruited *Senator Clinton, Hillary who co-chaired* with Senator John Cornyn (R-TX). [19] [17]

As you can see, USINPAC made sure that *no matter how we voted, H-1B visas and offshoring to India continued*.

LOBBIED FOR H-1BS AND US DEFENSE CONTRACTS

USINPAC claimed in 2003 it: *"stopped"* *Congressman's Tancredo's bill that would have killed the H-1B program, and "crushed"* Rep. Dan Burton candidacy for Chairman of the House Subcommittee on South Asia, because he was *"critical of India."* [18] How did they kill a bill, and *"crush"* a candidacy?

USINPAC helped India get money and access to buy US high-tech dual use civilian/military technology. For example, in 2004, India's Space Research chairman estimated India would spend $70 million buying dual use technology. [232]

Congress was pressured by USINPAC to open bids for *US defense contracts to India suppliers.* [413] Then, they proceeded to give *USINPAC members advice and legal help for obtaining US government contracts, federal grants, visas, and more.* [625] To win *"business opportunities for Indian Americans"* USINPAC aggressively sought awards for members, such as the Small Business Person of the Year, to create impressive credentials. USINPAC arranged *"exclusive meetings for its members"* with US senior government officials, and hosted sessions with our:

- *Department of Defense,*

- *Department of Energy,*

- *Department of Health & Human Services, and*

- *Department of Housing and Urban Development.* [625]

While our economy plummeted, they got rich. By 2007, USINPAC had 27,000 active members. It claimed *immigrants from India became the richest people in America* with median household income of $60,093 a year compared to $38,885 overall. They claimed to have 200,000 millionaires. [625] USINPAC even sends an annual delegation to India.

RARE AND OUTRAGEOUS HOUSE RESOLUTION 227

USINPAC's most prized lobbying win came in April 2005. _Congressmen Bobby Jindal co-sponsored a House Resolution 227_ bill with _Tom Davis that_ gave special recognition to Indian Institutes of Technology (IIT), and urged _all_ Americans to recognize how IIT graduates enriched our society. Never before in our nation's history was this type of special recognition lavished on a foreign university. USINPAC had such strong political clout, that Congress unanimously passed House Resolution 227. [342]

Jindal's House Resolution 227 was proudly displayed at a "Technology without Borders Global iit2005 Conference." The conference, co-chaired by Rajat Gupta Managing Director of McKinsey & Company (firm that hired Chelsea Clinton), encouraged IIT alumni to _help other IIT graduates use the India network to obtain subcontracting from the US government, to lend a hand to the India government, and more._ They planned a big PR campaign for "brand IIT." [523] US National Science Foundation Director of Industrial Innovation Kesh Narayanan, in charge of allocating a $100 million US research budget, was listed as an attendee. [485]

The recognition was sought to help universities in India solicit US government research grants. India also planned to use this resolution to get Corporate America to fund IIT research, and to get US universities to set up exchange programs. [342]

Our Congress was duped into positioning India to compete against the US globally! "Brand IIT: The IITian, today, is one of India's biggest exports to the US," a _dqindia.com_ 2005, article claimed: _"Before this, while IIT was among the top global education institutions, MIT or Stanford were still better recognized brands. This recognition may well establish the IITs in the same ranks as these institutes, and will help in establishing "Brand India" across the globe."_ [343] Congress should revoke this and promote "Brand USA."

NASSCOM – India's Software Lobby

India's lobby the *National Association of Software and Services Companies* (NASSCOM) <u>ultimate goal was to use H-1Bs to enable offshoring our high tech jobs to India</u>. "Making of a Software Superpower," a 1999 article said, "*NASSCOM has played a key role in propagating India as the destination for software services and development.*" [228] NASSCOM represented 850 companies globally. [404]

NASSCOM hired Hill & Knowlton an American PR company, to help lobby Congress. [404] Even though many American high tech workers were unemployed, from January to March 2003 *India "exported" 120,000 H-1B and 15,000 L1 visa workers to our country. India was concerned because Germany had decided to restrict the number of green cards and the United Kingdom was reconsidering its "fast track visa scheme." Parliamentary delegates from India traveled to the US to "lobby against bans on outsourcing."* [123]

Kiran Karnik, NASSCOM president in 2003, wasn't concerned when Americans tried to get a lower H-1B visa cap. He reasoned that a lower cap would have little impact because India already had so many H-1Bs in the US who could extend their visas. And, he pointed out that <u>for the long term the visas were becoming less important as the mix had shifted where offshoring was taking a much higher percentage of US jobs</u>. [96] His big concern was that we may stop offshoring BPO jobs to India. So, NASSCOM claimed that US banks, insurance companies and financial organizations benefited by offshoring BPO to India. He was "dismayed" that a bill in the Senate would restrict the offshoring of US government contract work. He called the requirement that our government contract work be done in the US an *"attack on free trade."* [87] To claim that offshoring was good for our economy, NASSCOM commissioned a McKinsey Global Institute "study" in 2003. IBM used this study to justify its offshoring plans. [100]

Leading up to our 2004 election, NASSCOM got help from The Indus Entrepreneurs (TiE–often referred to as "the India Mafia"), ITAA, and US executives on how to *"tackle the outsourcing issue."* [125] Their strategy: *"we are interacting with key decision and policy makers in the United States about the advantages of outsourcing to India will accrue to the sagging US economy."* [125]

Narayan Murthy, co-founder of Infosys, a large Indian outsourcing company, became president of NASSCOM. [601] In 2005, Murthy was recognized for his role when outsourcing became a political issue during our 2004 US presidential election. *India Today* called Murthy a "Prophet-at-Large." Murthy was number four on its list of "50 Power People." Infosys' outsourcing revenues reached $1 billion! [748] It would be interesting to find out what Murthy did during our 2004 election to be named a "Prophet-at-Large" by India. By March 2005, India's BPO revenues increased 46% to $3.6 billion. India added 70,000 new jobs. [127]

Indian American Center for Political Awareness

The publishers of *India Abroad* set up an "Indian American Center for Political Awareness" (IACPA) in 1994. IACPA created a Washington Leadership Program to place young Indian interns inside US Congressional Offices, and to send interns from the US to India.

On its website in 2005, IACPA was pleased when the H-1B cap was increased, and when *Congress was considering giving illegal immigrants "a temporary protected status under the Immigration Act to permit them to visit their relatives in Pakistan."* [425] How many IACPA members are in our country illegally?

India High Tech Council in Washington DC

By 2001, an Indian High Tech Council was set up in our nation's capital to lobby to benefit India. This council claimed to have more than 160 CEO members in the US including: Vasant Prabhu at *McGraw Hill*, Indira Nooyi president and COO at Pepsi, and Muktesh Pant chief marketing officer of Reebok. [366]

Need to End Lobbies with Foreign agendas

It is important that we build and maintain beneficial relations with other countries. However, lobbies that function to profit foreign countries violate the very core of our government which is supposed to represent US citizens. Foreign countries that use money to form lobbies that trump the will and interest of US citizens need to be stopped.

Immigrants who are found guilty of violating their US citizenship oath and harm our country to benefit their "mother country" should lose their US citizenship after any legal remedies are satisfied.

The "economic recovery" saw foreigners take more US jobs, while at the same time Americans lost millions of jobs. Moreover, these foreign workers continued their pattern of *"sending money back to their home country"* reported *The Wall Street Journal.* As demonstrated in the book, False Profits of False Prophets, these money transfers played a major role in our economic downturn. [912]

Chapter 6

Outsourcing Our Government!

Outsourcing may look like solid ground but it is sinking sand.

Not only have executives and foreign nations hijacked our government into passing laws that allowed them to outsource American jobs; *they have hijacked our government into funding offshore development, and into outsourcing and offshoring government work.* So the leaders of our team, "team USA," are giving the opposing team an open view into all our plays, our equipment, the money we are supposed to be getting paid, and even bringing in the competitors players for us to train. No wonder our competition is beating us. It's time to find new leaders.

While Congress set quota caps on the number of H-1Bs businesses could hire, it exempted US government, universities and other taxpayer funded organizations from the H-1B quota caps.

Our government also hired illegal aliens—some in sensitive jobs according to an article, "In Government, Too ... You'll Find Illegal Aliens in the Darndest Places." Our Social Security Administration gave out over 7 million "non-work" Social Security Numbers that were used by foreigners to obtain work illegally in the US. And, *our government instituted a tax code that prohibited disclosing the identity of these illegal aliens to the American public.* [637] This cover-up of illegal activity needs to stop.

Outsourcing Linked to War in Iraq

The government claims that huge defense budgets were to fund our troops. However, our government failed to tell us that outsourcing drives much of the costs of the war.

The war is a big moneymaker for contractors. William Nash, a retired Army general, called Pentagon hiring gun toting contractors "obscene." "Private Contractors Outnumber U.S. Troops in Iraq," a 2007 *Los Angeles Times* article said we had 160,000 troops in Iraq, and over 180,000 private contractors (<u>118,000 Iraqi, 43,000 other foreign, and only 21,000 US</u>). Plus, we were paying for an estimated 30,000 armed private security contractors. Brookings Institution scholar Peter Singer said, "*This is not the coalition of the willing. It is the coalition of the billing.*" [656]

War costs soared as contractors were accused of fraud, delivering faulty parts, and rigging bids. Companies avoided being banned by settling cases without admitting guilt. Though contractors in Iraq paid many penalties, the penalties appear insufficient to stop corruption. [575]

"State Department Waste in Iraq Cost Billions, Audit Finds," was a 2010 AP article. It reported that "*the volume and complexity of paperwork*" made it difficult to oversee contract billing resulting in the ***loss of billions of dollars*** [870]

"Up to $1Billion in U.S. Aid Winds Up in Taliban Coffers" a *Fox News* story reported that *only 10% of the money gets to the people who need it.* [895]

The withdrawal of our troops may actually increase defense spending in Iraq. According to a *Fox News* report "U.S. to Double Civilian Force in Iraq After Withdrawal," Obama plans to "*more than double the number of private security guards it has in Iraq.*" [871] Iraq needs to fund its own security.

Selling Outsourcing to Our Government

MITRE Corporation recommended outsourcing sensitive DOD software development to India–the same *year India deceived the US on its nuclear testing plans, which resulted in US sanctions against India!* A slide presentation promoting offshoring to our Department of Defense (DOD) was given by MITRE in 1998.

MITRE said our government needed to hire offshore programmers to get: *"Access to world-class talent not available internally."* On a later slide MITRE admitted that offshore programmers mostly worked on maintaining old software.

MITRE supplied a list of Indian outsourcing firms including:

- *HCL America, Information Management Resources, Mastech Systems, Overseas Technologies, Syntel, Tata Consultancy Services (TCS), and Wipro. Does MITRE's management have connections to India?*

MITRE named twelve other countries including Russia, but did not list their outsourcing companies.

To persuade our DOD to offshore, MITRE warned the US was facing a shortage of 200,000 IT workers by 2010. [138] From 1998 to 2010 is 12 years. There was ample time for us to educate enough Americans. Many of the foreign programmers only had a couple of Java classes which would take six months.

Billions in US Federal Government Defense contracts were awarded to MITRE for IT and engineering research for the Pentagon. [443] [138] MITRE claims to be, *"a not-for-profit organization chartered to work in the public interest,"* MITRE also managed Federally Funded Research and Development Centers. While MITRE's headquarters were in the US, it claimed to have over 60 sites worldwide. [444]

Foreign Aid Funds Competition

More than half of US aid goes to fund economic development in foreign countries. Foreign aid increased our trade imbalance. For example, from 1945 to 2002, we spent more than $2 trillion in foreign aid. In 2002 the US debt was $5 trillion. [401] We were taxed to fund our global competition!

Congressman Ron Paul also exposed how billons of our tax dollars fund risky loan guarantees for foreign countries through the Overseas Private Investment Corporation (OPIC). And, that *we fund the Export-Import Bank which finances risky loans to foreign governments and foreign businesses for projects that use American companies.* [287] *So, executives got our government to loan our tax money to foreign governments and to foreign businesses creating fake "emerging markets," which in turn used our money to buy products and services from the companies they ran.*

Federal Reserve Fiasco

A court order in 2011 forced U.S. Federal Reserve Chairman Ben S. Bernanke to release central bank documents. The bank did not want us to know that *the biggest discount borrowers during the 2008 banking crisis were foreign banks.* Ron Paul said Americans would be "outraged" when we found out that billions of dollars went to overseas banks when Americans were "losing their homes." [890]

The audit exposed $16 trillion in secret bank bailouts. US Senator Bernie Sanders said, *"No agency of the United States government should be able to bailout a foreign bank or corporation without the direct approval of Congress and the President."* Randal Wray, an economics professor, said, *"If such lending is not illegal, it should be...You close down fraudsters, period. The Fed and FDIC should have gone into the biggest banks immediately, replaced all top management, and ..."* [943] The spigot of our financial crisis is exposed.

Reclaim Control of Our Government

Our nation is on the brink of economic collapse. Companies receiving government outsourcing contracts should be American companies that employ only US citizens who pass rigorous background checks. Outsourcing government work to multinational businesses is too risky. They may have foreign conflicts of interest and may not disclose offshore interactions with foreign businesses or governments.

It is hard to believe that our Congress taxes us to fund insuring foreign banks and foreign competition. Americans invented the computer industry. We can produce our own programmers. If members of our government do not believe in us, then we need new leaders. In particular, we need to elect to Congress some of the outspoken critics of H-1B and offshoring legislation. Many worked diligently at their own expense trying to educate Congress and US businesses.

We need to stop excessive financial aid to foreign countries. No more money. In emergencies, if we are able, we should help with food, blankets, and medicine. If they want our money so that they can buy cheaper goods made in another country, let that country cover the cost.

Chapter 7

2004 Election Secrets

Then: US Citizens Selected Political Leaders

Now: Outsourcing Money Selects Political Leaders

Recall that foreign nations secretly engaged in illegal tampering with US elections using bipartisan gifting to promote outsourcing. For example, the FBI uncovered money China channeled to political parties to obtain *favorable trade policies (i.e. outsourcing)* in 1991. This fed China's appetite for US jobs. China gulped down our manufacturing jobs like a shark in a feeding frenzy. With the help of lobbies tossing in buckets full of bait, they were quite successful at buying favorable trade policies to catch the big fish to devour. China was not alone.

India's consumption of our programming jobs was stealthier. Like a giant python quietly encircling jobs with projected cost savings as lure, and then squeezing the life out of our economy. The South Asian Journalist Association (SAJA) website, *sajaforum.org* during our 2008 election revealed some intriguing history on our 2004 election. They warned US candidates *that opposing outsourcing is "an even greater risk this campaign season, given the increased clout of the community."* They cited John Kerry's "mistake" in 2004 as an example of their power saying: *"Congressional Democrats told him (Kerry) to cool down the anti-outsourcing rhetoric."* [822]

A SAJA post claimed that cardiologist Zach Zachariah, an immigrant from India, was a *"fundraising powerhouse of the Bush era (Bush 1 and 2 and Jeb Bush)"* raising $19 million for Republicans. [824] People don't raise millions of dollars for politicians unless they expect something in return.

According to SAJA people bundle campaign money because: *"Many bundlers secure government posts if their candidate wins, or have the inside track on lucrative business deals."* [824] Did a disproportionate number of immigrants from India get government posts and lucrative business deals from Bush 1 and 2? *Was the H-1B visa legislation passed under the first Bush Administration one of those lucrative deals?* The biggest employers of H-1Bs were India's outsourcing companies.

"You know it's sort of funny, before I got into politics, I always thought that the U.S. Senate and House were supposed to represent the U.S. of A. not India," wrote Chris Chatwood in a 2004 commentary titled, "A Great Sucking Sound from India." Chatwood claimed India wanted to stop the passage of state laws that would ban offshoring US government IT work to India, and said that Rep Joe Crowley encouraged India to appeal to Congress. [82]

War–A Diversion from Outsourcing

"Americans pre-occupied with the 800-pound gorilla called 'economy' and unless the 8,000-pound gorilla of terrorism overrides it, the 2004 Presidential election is likely to be fought on outsourcing alone. Bad news for India, 70% of whose $2.4 billion ITES revenues come from the US." was a quote by Norman J. Ornstein, a political commentator for American Enterprise Institute for Public Policy Research. [269] The war diversion worked as India accelerated the outsourcing of our professional programming, accounting and other jobs.

Outsourcing–A Big 2004 Political Issue

White collar American workers were hot under the collar from losing their jobs to foreign workers that they were forced to train. Previously offshoring protests were over lost blue collar jobs. We were told not to worry because that this left the better jobs for Americans. However, foreign nations used our blue collar jobs to gain a foothold, and then moved up the value chain link by link taking better and better jobs from us.

The Economics Times Online reported that alarming numbers of US software programmers earning $70,000 a year were being replaced by programmers in India willing to work for $18,000. [95]

A Gallup Poll in 2004 found that 83 out of every 100 of Americans polled said outsourcing was an important political issue. Almost half said they were worried that they or someone they knew may lose their job to a foreign worker. Similar results were reported by a 2004 Harris Poll with 84 out of every 100 Americans surveyed opposed to outsourcing. Hands down, Americans rejected Bush's economic advisor's claim that offshoring was good for our economy. [129]

Execs Delay Layoffs Until After Election

Executives put offshore plans *on hold until after the election to silence outsourcing protests*. The Vice Chairman of Wipro *claimed that US executives had no problem waiting six more months until the elections were over because they had held back on offshore outsourcing for two decades.* [109] Notice this means India's offshore outsourcing scheme was hatched in the early 1980's – well before the claims that the US had a worker shortage, and well before the dotcom bust which were both used to justify offshoring. After the election, a May 2, 2005, *US News and World Report* article, "Bangalore's Big Dreams," claimed that "the richest man in India" was Wipro Chairman Azim Premji a Muslim. [122]

Bush Administration Reassured India

George W. Bush was up for re-election. Our economy was in terrible shape as India exploited the dotcom crash to accelerate offshoring programming and other professional jobs.

When presidential hopeful John Kerry pledged to fight outsourcing of high-paying American jobs, India protested. Suspiciously, the Bush Administration was more anxious to reassure India than US citizens about outsourcing during the 2004 campaign. Why? Did India have a secret way to manipulate our election?

US AMBASSADOR TO INDIA REASSURED INDIA

Bush's US Ambassador to India, David Mulford, reassured India in March 2004, *"there could be no turning back"* because US business would call it *"intrusive government interference."* He said Kerry *"dug himself a hole so deep that he may actually have to come up with some legislation."* [120] And, he suggested that India educate US politicians on the benefits of offshoring so candidates would not raise it as a campaign issue. [120]

BUSH ADMINISTRATION TRADE REP REASSURED INDIA

"The Indian government and businesses have <u>won a major assurance from the Bush Administration on the issue of outsourcing</u>," reported a 2003, *Economic Times of India* article, "US Gives India Assurance on Outsourcing" by Chindanand Rajghatta. Bush's US Trade Representative, Robert Zellick, spent *"three hours of intensive talks with Indian Commerce Minister Arun Jaitley."* Jaitley warned that the proposed state bans would impede India's free access to US markets. American workers lost, and India won. [86] Outsourcing is not "free trade"–it is a dispossession of US jobs and technology. Moreover, India has trade barriers.

BUSH SECRETARY OF STATE COLIN POWELL REASSURED INDIA

"Where in the World is Our Colin Powell," asked the *HireAmericanCitizens.org* website.

They found a surprising answer. A blog post from the *New York Times in New Delhi* featured a visit by US Secretary of State Colin Powell, and claimed he was there to reassure Prime Minister Atal Bihari Vajpayee and other leaders in India that Republicans were pro-outsourcing during the 2004 presidential campaign.

In his meetings, Powell _requested that India lower its trade barriers_ to help ease outsourcing protests which created problems for US politicians. [325] Now that exposes how off track our government had gone. American workers wanting to keep their jobs so they could pay their mortgage and keep a roof over their family's head, and food on the table for their kids was a problem for our politicians!

Powell assured the government of India that if Bush remained in office US outsourcing would continue.

Even worse, to help address the "trade" imbalance, Powell offered to sell India advanced US space and nuclear technology, under the condition, *"India imposes controls so that the technology is not passed on to other countries."* [325] This was a bad deal for the US for many reasons.

Powell also reassured students in India that US outsourcing would continue–even after they accused our country of arbitrarily using force, and showed no empathy for Americans their age fighting in a war to defend our nation. So, let's see, he promised college students in India US jobs that should go to young American college students. [325] And we were taxed to pay for his trip?

Government Withheld Outsourcing Report!

An outsourcing study commissioned by Congress was secretly withheld from voters until after our 2004 election. [407]

An *EETimes* article claimed the report released after the election was cut from 365 pages to only 12 pages, and data exposing outsourcing damage were removed such as:

- *Design engineers in China and India were paid 80% less than Americans; and offshoring jeopardized our technology leadership.*

- *"Most of the 4,000 to 5,000 employees of US companies in India represent jobs lost to the US economy." And, returning H-1Bs helped India compete against us in our own technologies. [544]*

An "EEs Fatalistic About Design Offshoring," *EETimes* article referred to the *"Quashed report,"* and said American engineers were concerned that offshoring design work for short term gains jeopardized US technology leadership. [543]

"Political Appointees Re-Write Commerce Department Report on Offshore Outsourcing: Original Analysis is Missing From Final Version" an article in *Manufacturing & Technology News* said the report released in 2005 was altered to favor outsourcing.

- *The original report exposed that the driver for offshoring was a* <u>*surplus of workers in India, not a shortage of Americans.*</u>

- *The original had trend charts and offshore plans for American companies such as IBM, HP, and Microsoft. [407]*

Our tax dollars paid $335,000, for this report which concluded: *"it was not possible to determine whether the shift of U.S. work to non-U.S. locations resulted in jobs losses for U.S. workers..."* [407] Now that is absurd. A little common sense would tell you that if you lay off a US worker and hire a foreign worker that is one loss, do this a million times and that adds up to a million lost jobs. The math is far from complicated. We should get a refund.

India Confident Despite US Citizens' Protests

Why were Indian outsourcers so confident during our 2004 election? PV Kannan, the CEO of a call center in Bangalore said: *"I believe smart Indian business-persons are entrenched in the American market and their savvy "lobbying" will counterbalance the nay sayers."* [158]

H-1Bs were not supposed to take jobs from US citizens. But they did. Displaced Americans formed H-1Bs protest websites:

- *The Programmers Guild*
- *The Organization for the Rights of American Workers*
- *zazona.com*
- *techsunite.org*
- *h1bprotest.com*
- *HireAmericanCitizens.org*

Even so, BG Mahesh of *bpoindia.org* was not worried about these sites: *"Americans understand numbers very well. At the end of the day they want to see good numbers on the balance sheet. So I doubt these sites will have an adverse effect on outsourcing."* [158]

Who was making outsourcing look good on the balance sheets? Foreign workers in our accounting firms. For example:

- *Arthur Andersen, an accounting giant, was felled by the Enron scandal. At the time of its demise Andersen had morphed into a multinational with 85,000 employees. Only 28,000 of its employees worked in the US! So for every one employee in the United States, Andersen had about three overseas. But that's not all. Andersen employed H-1Bs, so many of its US workers were not US citizens.*

Ernst & Young and the Indo-American Chamber of Commerce in Mumbai jointly produced a "study" predicting 50% growth for India's offshoring in 2005. Their prediction mirrored NASSCOM's. Did Congress know that Ernst & Young employed H-1Bs and offshored, and that Ranjan Biswas, an Ernst & Young partner, helped produce the study? [111]

Defending Outsourcing During 2004 Election

Two months before the 2004 election, Columbia University professor Jagdish Bhagwati wrote: "Muddled and Maddening" an article published in the *Wall Street Journal*. He said John Kerry was silly for calling executives offshoring to India "Benedict Arnolds." *Bhagwati was surprised Kerry made such "gaffes" because Howard Dean and Dick Gephardt criticized outsourcing and were eliminated from the race.* [524] How was India eliminating candidates who opposed outsourcing?

> Jagdish Bhagwati's book, *In Defense of Globalization*, criticized the US for *"excessive intellectual property protection at the WTO."* [257] Born in India, Bhagwati has been an advisor to the UN, the WTO, and to India's Finance Minister. [258] He went to graduate school in the US and got a Ph.D. from MIT.

According to Bhagwati, Kerry's advisors had him acting like a protectionist to his constituents while cunningly giving the opposite story *"to those who matter."* [524]

"How does one forgive him (Kerry) *his pronouncements on outsourcing...?"*, Bhagwati asked for Kerry's, *"truly disturbing sin of commission."* He worried that if elected *"Kerry cannot totally jilt his constituents."* [524] Who does Bhagwati think a president of the US is commissioned to serve?

Bhagwati made fun of Kerry for not distinguishing between US companies that built offshore operations, and those that hired outsourcing companies for "services" such as reading x-rays, or preparing tax returns. Bhagwati claimed the latter job losses were "miniscule" with only about 100,000 US jobs lost per year, and if it increased to a million lost jobs a year it would still be "ludicrous" for us to be alarmed.

The day after Bhagwati's article was in the *Wall Street Journal*, *The Hindu Business Line* published an article: "Expert Assails Kerry's Trade Policy." It called Bhagwati an "expert" on outsourcing, and criticized Kerry. The author quipped that *Kerry should listen to Bill Clinton*, and insisted that Kerry is really a free trade advocate. [525]

Notice India thought only "free trade" i.e. pro-offshoring candidates would be on our election ballots.

John Pardon, a US IT professional who has been published in *Computerworld* and quoted in the *New York Times*, criticized Bhagwati's "Muddled and Maddening" article. He said it was a *"mean-spirited and non-intellectual"* attack intended *"to undermine the credibility and integrity of American free trade and outsourcing critics in the media and politics .... Bhagwati ignores the real criticisms of outsourcing and attempts to obscure the issues by creating a ridiculous caricature of the free trade critique."* [260]

Bhagwati wanted H-1Bs working in the US to pay taxes to India. He called this "taxing the brain drain." [258] He also wrote an article, "Borders Beyond Control," advocating the United States not try to control immigration, but rather cope with it. [258]

Following the election, *Times of India* in New Delhi reported Bhagwati, was eager to reclaim his Indian 'nationality' as a dual citizen because he felt an *"obligation to my country."* He wanted to vote in India's elections, and pay taxes to India. He said India's diaspora were "doing wonderful things" for India. And people were *"quite happy to be hyphenated Americans."* [886]

Bhagwati, like several immigrants from India became rich promoting outsourcing American jobs to workers from India.

Electronic Vote Tampering Risks

Skilled programmers know that there are infinite ways to tamper with computerized voting. For example, weeks of tests could show voting machines work perfectly. However hidden in the code could be other code that changes the counting process only during the high voting times only on Election Day. For example, on Election Day the program code could take every 5th vote for candidate A and count it for candidate B instead. Without a paper trail no one would know.

Computer security experts warned repeatedly that electronic voting posed an unacceptably high risk of foreign tampering. Despite these warnings our government spent millions setting up electronic voting systems.

The Pentagon developed an electronic voting system to enable overseas internet voting in 2004. Independent experts analyzed the system and *warned that the system could be hacked by foreign governments, terrorists, or others wanting to manipulate US election results.* Moreover, they said electronic systems violate voters' privacy rights by keeping records of how people voted. Nonetheless, the Pentagon planned to use the system. [223]

Aggressive lobbying by manufacturers of electronic voting machines trumped security concerns. Some of these companies employ H-1Bs, and are members of the ITAA lobby that resisted providing a paper audit trail claiming it would only give *"a false sense of security."* [20]

It's risky to have H-1Bs program our voting machines that record and tally US election results. H-1Bs may alter votes to elect politicians who promise to: continue the H-1B program, grant green cards, outsource big government contracts, give US financial aid to their country, grant amnesty, or other favors.

India Decides Who Controls Whitehouse!?

The South Asia Analysis Group published a strategy paper by Hari Sud, a graduate of Punjab University and the University of Missouri, on how to protect India's outsourcing during our 2004 election. Sud, who lived in Canada, said India should use the US media to put a positive spin on outsourcing. [131]

Sud said that if Bush was kept in the Whitehouse outsourcing to India would continue. [131] He told India that Kerry's proposal could be tied up in committees and hearings for years before being voted on. Sud advised, *"It is in the best interest of India to tame the debate now than later."* [131]

The shocker was Sud's call to action: *"The two political parties are expressing two different visions on how to handle the BPO flight of jobs to India... Which of the two is a better evil for India has to be decided by Government of India. It has to be decided fast. The party, which controls the Whitehouse, will control the outcome ..."* [131] Why does Sud think India has the power to decide who controls our Whitehouse!?

- *Could it be electronic voting? By 1999, Indians took almost a third of the programming jobs in the US! At less than 1% of our population they had 33% of our IT jobs?* [213] *Following the dotcom crash **9 of every 10 of new US programming jobs went to H-1Bs in 2001**?* [143] *US executives laid off over a million Americans, and hired 991,000 foreign visa workers.* [397]

Sud's solution, "the trade issue has to be addressed in such a way that a few high paying jobs in America are made dependent on trade with India." [131] Ergo we see big executive bonuses dependent on outsourcing to India.

Chapter 8

Media 4th Branch of

Government?

From freedom of speech to "politically correct" control.

The birth of our nation was paved by a free press. Newspapers and books, such as <u>Common Sense</u> by Thomas Paine, shone the light guiding our pathway to freedom. We need timely and accurate information in areas vital to our economic, cultural, and national security interests for democracy to work. A free uncompromised media breathes life into our democracy. With it our freedom thrives and our nation excels. Media is *"often called the fourth branch of government"* because of the power it exerts over political races and politicians. [1026]

Our political system only works when we are informed voters, and in turn when our politicians honor their oath of office and carry out the wishes of Americans they represent. Media's greatest influence is at the beginning of the race. Media can propel a runner to the front of the pack. Media can destroy candidates. Clever choices of words can obscure the truth, and make a bad candidate look good, and good candidate look bad. Media owners with political agendas can trip candidates right out of the gate. By predicting winners and losers, media creates winners and losers. Corrupt media instead of informing us, manipulates us.

Our Media Has Been Hijacked!

Following election news in the US is like one of those stories where you get lost in the wilderness. You take a trail walk all day then find yourself back where you started. Then you take a different trail, but once again you end up at the same place. We want to elect politicians who will work for Americans. Yet, following our media just takes us in a circle and we get another pro-outsourcing, pro-amnesty politician.

"White House Boasts: We 'Control' News Media," a 2008 *WND* article reported that Anita Dunn, Obama's chief campaign manager, claimed that Obama's campaign *"focused on "making" the news media cover certain issues while rarely communicating anything to the press unless it was "controlled.""* She explained that they did videos *"because it was a way for us to get our message out without having to actually talk to reporters."* [804]

"Media Blackout on Obama Eligibility Dates Back to November," a 2009 *Canada Free Press* article by Douglas Hagmann and Judi McLeod, reported, *"our investigation has uncovered both direct and indirect evidence of threats being made against some of the nation's top radio and television personalities."* They claimed that the threats came *"from the very top in all cases,"* and that *"the nature of this manipulation, and the extent of the threats against journalists, should shock even the most well grounded."* [803]

Who's at the Top- Who Owns our Media?

Especially surprising is how much of our news ownership has been bought by foreign born George Soros, foreign born Rupert Murdoch, foreign Saudi Prince Al Waleed, and a few multinational corporations. These are not owners whose history gives a deep appreciation for our heritage and the generations that built this country through hard work and personal sacrifice.

Soros Bought Media and Founded "Shadow Party"

Why does George Soros spend so much to control our media? You find the answer in the prologue of his 2006 book, The Age of Fallibility: "*The main obstacle to a stable and just world order is the United States. …Changing the attitude and policies of the United States remains my top priority.*" Hungarian born Soros came to our country in 1956. He became a hedge fund billionaire. [910]

Soros funds Democrats, but is secretive because: "*the Democratic Party does not stand for the policies that I advocate: indeed, if it did, it could not be elected. I prefer to be above politics.*" [910]

George Soros bought media influence in: "*the New York Times, Washington Post, the Associated Press, NBC and ABC.*" [909] A 2011 *Fox News* story, "Why Don't We Hear About Soros' Ties to Over 30 Major News Organizations?" reported conflict of interests where Soros funded journalists to promote his agenda. It also claimed Soros gave $8 billion to Open Society Foundations, a network of 30 international foundations, and spent "*$27 million trying to defeat President Bush in 2004.*" [908]

"SHADOW PARTY" SECRETIVE

"*Soros founded and organized the Shadow Party personally,*" according to a 2006 book, The Shadow Party: How George Soros, Clinton, Hillary, and Sixties Radicals Seized Control of the Democratic Party. It claimed: "*If Americans understood the intentions of the Shadow Party organizers, they would recoil in revulsion and reject its overtures. For these reasons, the Shadow Party network must proceed by stealth. It must (and does) use secretive, deceptive, and extra-constitutional means to achieve its objectives. It must infiltrate government bureaucracies, corrupt public officials and manipulate the press. And it must conceal who and what it is.*" [933] The book quotes Eli Pariser, head of the Soros funded MoveOn PAC, who said of the Democrat Party in 2004, "*Now it's our party. We bought it, we own it.*" [933]

SOROS TACTICS

"The Capitalist Threat," written by Soros in 1997, gives insight into his tactics: *"Societies derive their <u>cohesion from shared values. The values are rooted in culture, religion, history, and tradition.</u> When a society does not have boundaries, where are the shared values to be found? I believe there is only one possible source: the concept of the open society itself."* [932]

"George Soros: Open Society and Open Borders," in *newsmax.com* reported, The Open Society Institute provides funds to: *"Democracy Alliance, <u>MoveOn.org</u>, America Coming Together, America Votes, The Center for American Progress, and other <u>leftist front organizations, which advocate open borders for the United States–not for other nations.</u>."* The article surmised: *"Essential to an open society is <u>destruction of the nation-state authority, family structure, and religious beliefs.</u>"* [909] Did Soros take his strategy from Joseph Stalin who said, *"America is like a healthy body and its resistance is threefold: its patriotism, its morality, and its spiritual life. If we can undermine these three areas, America will collapse from within."*

"*Guide to the George Soros Network,*" on *discoverthenetworks.org* lists groups that receive Open Society money such as: <u>*La Raza, Amnesty International, ACLU, The Arab American Institute,*</u> *plus many more.* [936] Its grants paid legal defense for illegal aliens, and paid journalists to write empathetic articles *"to sway public opinion in favor of illegal aliens and open borders."* [909] What more subversive and effective way to destroy our nation's *"cohesion from shared values"* than by flooding our nation with people who do not share our *"culture, religion, history and tradition."* [932]

Soros strokes protests and conflicts writing about *"intolerable inequities"*. [932] Isn't it ridiculous for a hedge fund billionaire to fault hardworking middle class Americans for economic inequities?

"Soros Warns of 'Riots,' 'Brutal' Clampdowns & Possible Total Economic Collapse," a January 2012 story in the Blaze said Soros was almost "gleeful" when he talked about the prospect of Occupy Wall Street riots. He said, *"It will be an excuse for cracking down and using strong-arm tactics to maintain law and order, which, ... could bring about a repressive political system, a society where individual liberty is much more constrained, which would be a break with the tradition of the United States."* [1027] Interesting the article said that in 1992 Soros "helped crash England's economy." [1027]

And, who is funding Occupy that could bring about *"a repressive political system"* in our country? Guess. "George Soros Funds Occupy Wall Street," was a 2011 article by Matthew Vadum. [1028] He said Soros co-founded *"ultra-secretive Democracy Alliance, a billionaires' club"* that wants to radically transform America. And that Soros' is *"a currency manipulator with an insider-trading conviction."* [1028]

"Soros and Liberal Groups Seeking Top Election Posts in Battleground States," by *The Washington Times* in June 2011, warned his "Secretary of State Project" goal was to *"put Democrats in charge of state election offices"* that decide who can vote and "<u>which ballots are counted and which are not</u>." [935] Stalin quote: *"Those who cast the votes decide nothing. Those who count the votes decide everything."*

"Billionaire George Soros Trying to Stack the Courts, Critics Say," was a 2011 Fox News story where an attorney, Colleen Pero, warned, *"...they think they can get their agenda through by <u>taking over the courts</u>."* She did a study that discovered Soros' Open Society gave millions to *"reshape the judiciary,"* and wanted judges to be selected by committee not elected by citizens. [934]

Obama's carefully crafted speeches set the stage for Soros' Open Society by promoting amnesty, claiming we are no longer a Christian nation, and apologizing for our history.

Media "Mum on Amnesty" for Felons!

"Media Mum on Amnesty of Illegal Aliens Who Commit Identity Felonies," was a September 2012 report by *NumbersUSA*. What Obama doesn't want you to know, and what the media isn't telling you is that Obama's Deferred Action for Childhood Arrivals (DACA) amnesty is telling adult illegals that they can apply for work permits even if they committed felony crimes of identity theft or fraud. An immigration attorney said our government understands such crimes were "*a necessary part of living in the shadows.*" [1029] Two months later, "Over 50,000 Illegal Aliens Received Amnesty Work Permits under Obama's DACA Program" and 273,000 were in "*the final stages of the approval process.*" [1044] *Obama is helping illegal aliens take jobs that should go to young Americans who need jobs to repay college loans!*

Rupert Murdoch our Elections & Media

"Rupert Murdoch Calls for Amnesty for 'Law-Abiding' Illegal Immigrants" was a 2010 *cnsnews.com* report. Illegal aliens are not law-abiding. Murdoch, an immigrant from Australia, was a big Bush supporter. His family owns controlling shares of News Corp. [854] Why are foreign born billionaires promoting open borders? They feign empathy for illegal aliens. Their philanthropy is twisted. They hold onto their wealth and give ours away.

Murdoch testified to the House Judiciary Subcommittee on Immigration that he "*joined Mayor Bloomberg in organizing the Partnership for a New American Economy ...so we can continue to compete in the 21ˢᵗ century global economy.*" He said it was too costly–$285 billion to deport illegals. Steven Camarota, director of research at the Center for Immigration Studies disagreed with Murdoch. He testified that illegals take jobs from Americans, and "*the wage loss is 12 times bigger than the benefits.*" [878]

Saudi Prince Buys US Media Control

"Saudi Prince Al Waleed Goes Spending Again," a 1997, *Time* article, reported he bought: $400 million of News Corp, $300 million of Motorola, and $146 million of Netscape. Why? He said, *"I want to concentrate on communications, technology, entertainment and news. ...This is the future. News Corp is the only truly global news and entertainment company. Netscape is strongly involved with the Internet. Motorola is very global in telephones and satellites. These companies are going to play a crucial role."* [852] What crucial role?

"The Prince and The Media," a 2001 WND report said the Prince owned: $2.05 billion of AOL, $50 million of Disney (Controls ABC and other global media), and 3% of News Corp (Fox News, the New York Post, and other media). [267]

"Saudi Prince, Now Part Owner of Murdoch's News Corp., Influences Fox News," critics were alarmed about his influence:

■ *2001 owned 3% –Fox News praised Giuliani when he rejected a $10 million check from the Prince after the Prince blamed the 9/11 attacks on US policies, not the Saudi terrorist hijackers. Then...*

■ *2005 owned 5.4%– An investigative journalist, Joseph Trento complained Fox edited out his comment that Saudis finance Al-Qaeda. Trento said the Prince "has personally donated huge amounts of money to the families of Palestinian suicide bombers."*

■ *2010 owned 7% (largest shareholder outside Murdoch family). ThinkProgress.org reported that in an interview on Fox the Prince said he wanted to influence our politics because his country's GDP relies on selling oil to the US. The article asserted the Prince used media control to keep us dependent on buying Saudi oil. [853]*

In 2010, Murdoch teamed up with Saudi Prince Al Waleed to launch 'Arabic Fox News.' [854] This Saudi Prince was reported to have financial ties to the *Bush Family*, the *Carlyle Group*, and *Citigroup*. [854]

Corporations Bought Media Control

A handful of corporate executives control most of what we see on TV from news to entertainment. Many hired H-1Bs and offshored our jobs.

- *General Electric bought NBC stock.*
- *News Corporation bought Fox stock.*
- *Walt Disney Company bought ABC stock plus 8 more channels.*
- *Viacom bought CBS and UPN stocks plus eleven more channels.*
- *Time Warner bought shares in 9 channels.* [340]

Multinationals that own our media can make huge political "contributions." Why? They get much of the money back when political campaigns pay for running ads.

During our 2008 election TV/Movies/Music industry contributions almost doubled jumping from $14 million in 2004 to $26 million in 2008. They used a bipartisan strategy giving to Republicans and Democrats so they are in control no matter which party wins. [268]

Politically Correct = Control

Do ratings and polls reflect what we think? Or, do they lead us around like a bull with a politically correct ring in its nose?

During our elections we are told that unless we vote for candidates favored by the media that we are throwing away our vote. Is that true? How many of your family and friends have enough money to make big political contributions?

Are candidates that raise millions of dollars going to look out for you, or for lobbies and rich people making big contributions?

Reclaiming our Media & Elections

What good is the media if it is compromised and being used to promote outsourcing our jobs, and illegally crossing our borders?

A few rich people and foreign nations were able to keep us in the dark about their political manipulations because they didn't just buy US political influence; *they also bought control of our media.* [173] They tell us what is "politically correct." Their strategy is to marginalize, discredit, and demean Americans who object to outsourcing and amnesty.

Staged "politically correct" media coverage is pretend news. It is used to suppress the truth. We have become like the people in the children's story "The Emperor's New Clothes" where everyone was afraid to say: "The emperor is not wearing any clothes!"

We need TV coverage for qualified candidates who have not accepted huge political "contributions" that compromise their objectivity. We need reporters who will seek out the real stories and expose people who use money to exert too much power over our elections and setting our government policies.

> Should a global network supply the data used in US political ads to influence our elections? TNS Media Intelligence, a network headquartered in New York, spans 70 countries. This network sold political ad data: *"key decision makers from local campaigns to Fortune 100 companies came to TNSMI/CMR for reliable political ad data, as they did in past election cycles."* [266]

Chapter 9

US 2008 Election Who Really

Won?

"Change" can be a nebulous thing.

W as the big winner from Obama's 2008 election India? "Indian PM Becomes President Obama's First State Guest," a 2009 article, by Ravi Khanna wrote, *"New Delhi will be looking to see if Mr. Obama wants to sustain the deepened relationship forged under former president George Bush."* [788]

"$200M-a-day Cost of Obama's Trip to India will be picked up by US Taxpayers," a 2010 report noted the Obama took this trip while we were facing record deficits. [897] Among other expenses, we were billed for *"the complete booking of the 570 room Taj Mahal Hotel for his security entourage."* They were careful not to draw attention to Bangalore or Hyderabad where outsourcing and offshoring by US firms such as Intel, Cisco, Google, IBM, and Microsoft had secretly transferred not only jobs, but $60 billion a year in IT revenues from the US to India. [897] About 3,000 people accompanied Obama! [1024] If you are not happy about airport body scanners, guess what– "Naked Body Scanner Manufacturer's CEO (Deepak Chopra) Obama's Guest on Trip to India." Chopra and Obama met with entrepreneurs in Mumbai. [913] What did we get for funding this trip? *The Times of India* proclaimed, *"Obama acknowledges decline of US dominance."* [898]

Obama Made "India-born" Vivek Kundra CIO!

As mentioned earlier USINPAC wanted a "US cyber policy" post. Obama created a new federal Chief Information Officer (CIO) post. "India-born executives leading candidates for Obama Tech Job" a *Times of India* article reported, "*Neither the Obama transition team nor the two executives would comment on their potential selection.*" [817] Obama picked Vivek Kundra to be our nation's first CIO. [798] Kundra's family moved to the US from India when he was eleven. [816] This post gave unprecedented access to sensitive strategic federal computer networks.

Obama Named Rajiv Shah Foreign Aid Chief

Obama picked Rajiv Shah, a 36 year old medical doctor whose family immigrated to the US from India "*to run the U.S. Agency for International Development.*" Obama planned to "*double the amount of money spent on foreign aid.*" [836] Why would Obama pick a medical doctor with close connections to India to dole out US Aid? Isn't this a conflict of interest given India has been a major recipient? And, why are we funding foreign development?

Indian-Americans Got "Key Legal Posts"

An *India West News Report*, "Obama Names Indian Americans to Key Legal Posts," said: Obama named Preeta Bansal to "*serve as general counsel and senior policy advisor in the Obama-Biden administration's Office of Management and Budget.*" And, Obama "*appointed Georgetown University law professor Neal Katyal to the post of principal deputy solicitor general.*" (Katyal defended Osama bin Laden's driver before the Supreme Court in 2006.) "*In an e-mail, Kayal told India-West he could not comment on the appointment, in keeping with a directive from the Department of Justice.*" [797] Both Bansal and Katyal had clerked for a US Supreme Court Justice. [797] Do the demographics of these clerks mirror our population?

"President Obama's Team India"!?

Astoundingly, *NDTV Profit*, New Delhi, India posted a YouTube video, "President Obama's Team India" September 2010. You may want to watch this video, if they don't remove it.

"We have these Indians now in Washington, and if India needs something you just pick up the phone and call Team India. We did a count and there are almost 15 people of Indian origins in this particular administration. Which is a wonderful thing.... We get very excited when we see that." The host announced India instituted a special award for "Excellence in International Governance," and said, *"the award goes to President Obama's Team India."* [944]

Obama's "Team India" members traveled to India to receive the award:

- The host said to Vivek Kundra, *Obama's Chief Information Officer:* "*__Vivek your job is to make all this official information transparent__*." [944] *Wasn't Vivek supposed to protect our federal computers from foreign access?*

- *Farah Pandith, Obama's Special Rep for Muslim Communities,* commented about her post: *"the job that was created for me at the State Department"*

Three members accepted the award via televised messages.

- *Ro Khanna Deputy Assistant Secretary of Domestic Operations of the US & Foreign Commercial Services Department of Commerce International Trade Administration, whose grandfather spent 4 years in jail fighting for India's independence, said:* "History has now come full circle." [944] Isn't he confusing America with Britain? Americans never jailed his grandfather. [944]

- *Preeta Bansal, Vice Chair Administrative Conference of the US.*

- *Richard Verna, Assistant Secretary of State for Legislative Affairs, US Department of State.*

Obama's Campaign Promises to "India Abroad"

Was Obama fulfilling campaign promises when he made his "Team India" appointments? Look at what campaign promises Obama made to foreign students and visa workers.

In an *India Abroad* February 2008 issue, Obama told foreign students from India: *"My relationship with the community stretches back to my days as a student. This bond is strong and deep because it is in part personal. Like so many Indian Americans, my father arrived in America* ___without money___, *but with a student visa and a determination to live his dreams."* Obama said, *"As President, I will* __double our foreign assistance.__*"* [786] Promising to double foreign student grants when many Americans cannot afford college is appalling. *Note that Obama was making campaign promises to foreigners who cannot legally vote!*

Obama told *"his own family's immigrant story."* (Obama father was not an immigrant–he came to the US on a *non-immigrant* student visa). Obama promised amnesty to millions: *"Too often, restrictions at our borders have prevented entry for many students and family members who seek nothing more than opportunity and reunification with loved ones. In the process,* __we have restricted the promise of America for millions__ *of hard-working, law-abiding individuals who advance our nation's economy and potential through strong families, excellence in education and achievement, and* __personal faith__*."* [786] Hindus and Muslims?

Few Americans would have voted for Obama if they knew he promised in *India Abroad* that if elected, he would, *"open up the federal government, put more information on-line, and create* __a new level of transparency__ *so that we change the way business is done in Washington."* He promised *"transparency"* of our confidential federal government information to non-citizens!

And, Obama told them that *he voted for the US-India* __nuclear deal__. [786]

Foreign Election Tampering

Millions of foreigners living in our country had opportunity and motives to illegally influence our election:

- ■   *First, there were the vast numbers of foreign students who want us to pay for their education, and who want work visas.*

- ■   *Second, there were millions of foreigners on temporary non-immigrant work visas who want green cards.*

- ■   *Third, there were 12-30 million illegal aliens who wanted amnesty*

Foreigners living in our country could show up at political rallies, and beat the campaign trail masquerading as US citizens. Because of poor election security, millions may have voted.

The *National Association of Foreign Student Advisors* (NAFSA) wanted to repeal the law that requires foreign students return to their country after college. [186] According to Dr. Matloff, NAFSA *"is one of the most aggressive lobbying groups on immigration issues on Capitol Hill ...they once had the audacity to try to pressure me not to testify before Congress."* [186] Outrageously, they wanted to tax us to pay for their college, and in turn they want to take our jobs!

Immigration Voice picketed our Capitol, *met with our politicians,* and filed lawsuits in 2007 because of green card backlogs. H-1Bs protested the limit of 140,000 green cards per year, and the 7% *limit per country.* [642] Yet, H-1Bs are <u>here on *non-immigrant visas*</u>. And, green cards are only supposed to be granted if there are no qualified Americans. We had high unemployment, so *it is not likely that we had any jobs that could not be filled by citizens.* Protestors said companies *"dangle the hope of permanent residency"* [642] to recruit them. They tried to keep below the radar of H-1B critics. They felt *"demoralized."* [642] How do they think the Americans whose jobs they took felt when they lost their jobs, homes, and health insurance because of H-1B visa fraud? Company severance Agreements denied US citizens a voice.

Vote for H1-B, or Vote for H-1B, or Vote for H1-B

What kind of choice was that?

Loss of our jobs to foreign workers was a hot political issue. So how did our presidential race narrow down to three that were pro H-1B visas, according to a February 2008 *InfoWorld* article, "Clinton, McCain and Obama on H-1B Visas" [801] McCain's campaign website incredulously claimed hiring H-1Bs created jobs for Americans: *"Hiring skilled foreign workers to fill critical shortages benefits not only innovative companies, but also our economy. For every foreign worker hired, corporations generally hire five to ten additional American workers."* [800]

USINPAC "Coalitions of Minorities" Strategy

As reported earlier USINPAC in 2003 proclaimed that they blocked Rep Tom Tancredo's bill to end the H-1B visa program.

USINPAC donated to candidates from both parties seeking *"favorable policies"* benefiting Indian-Americans. They held fundraisers for: Chet Culver the Gov. of Iowa, Hillary Clinton, Joe Biden, Tom Davis, Bobby Jindal, and many more. [625]

Did our candidates know that USINPAC also held meetings with: the Prime Minister of India, <u>American Voice</u>, India's Minister of Science and Technology, and more? [625]

USINPAC's "think-tank" strategy conceived in 2002, to get their people elected was to form "<u>*coalitions with other minorities in the country–African Americans, Hispanics and other people of Asian descent.*</u>" [521] Ironically, H-1Bs from India took minority job opportunities that should have gone to US minorities. Yet, they planned to use the people they displaced to get US political power. They promoted anti-white racism to minorities. And, they promoted white guilt to impressionable young white Americans.

Latinos Flipped Battleground States for Obama

"In Key States, Latino Vote Fueled Obama's Victory," in the *nydailynews.com* reported *that "Latinos helped Democrats flip the battleground states of Colorado, Nevada, New Mexico, and Florida."* [784] Frank Sharry, Director of <u>American Voice</u> a group pressuring Congress for another amnesty said: "Boy, it's just really hard to vote for a party that says they're going to deport your loved ones." *Gustavo Garcia said, "It totally makes me happy... I think that this election was the **election of the minorities."** * [784] Did the 1986 amnesty decide our 2008 election?

97% of Arabs & 94% of South Asians Vote Obama

Obama had nearly unanimous support from Muslims, Hindus, and Buddhists. The Asian American Legal Defense and Education Fund released its exit poll survey results that showed *"South Asians almost unanimously voted for Barack Obama."* The results for Michigan showed, *"Arab and South Asian American voters gave Obama the most support, with 97% and 94% of those polled."* Chinese Americans voted 76% for Obama. [831]

The National Asian American Survey also reported that Indian voters overwhelmingly supported Obama. And, *"Those who participate in the politics of their home countries in some manner are actually more likely to vote in the United States than those who do not."* Professor Karthick Ramakrishnan, said, *"it is understandable that interest in the homeland will help foster participation in the U.S."* The report said, *"Indians are slow to assimilate in America."* [827]

After the election, a SAJA post quoted Rajen Anand, *"I feel proud of America today that we have elected a man of color."* Ironically, Anand also said, *"The older generation has always been very prejudiced; <u>Indians are extremely prejudiced against people of color.</u> That is still there and it will take some time to overcome that."* [826]

SAJA – "Disproportionate" Election Influence

What's SAJA? It is the South Asian Journalist Association (SAJA). The website, *sajaforum.org*, revealed insights into 2008 election activities hidden from most Americans, such as: South Asians *"(approx. three million voters, non-voters, etc) played a disproportionate role (multiple roles, actually) Watch for efforts to woo the community and its money."* [819] Our elections are for US citizens to decide, not South Asia. Were the *"non-voters, etc."*, non-citizens?

"Hillary Clinton (D-Punjab)" a document that exposed her investments in outsourcing and India was circulated by the Obama campaign according to a June 15, 2007, SAJA post. They *warned Obama's campaign that opposing outsourcing is "an even **greater risk this campaign season**, given the increased clout of the community."* And noted Obama was making the same mistake as John Kerry when, *"Congressional Democrats told him (Kerry) to **cool down the anti-outsourcing rhetoric**."* [822] What risk? Were they threatening candidates who opposed outsourcing? Obama quickly squelched the outsourcing data on Hillary, and apologized for the "screw-up." Obama said the outsourcing criticism *"didn't reflect the fact that I have longstanding support and friendships within the Indian-American community."* [820] [638]

"Obama Tells South Asian Audience, "I am a Desi"–SAJA defined "Desi" as *"a colloquial term that describes South Asian immigrants."* [833] *Obama claimed to be an immigrant?!* A South Asians for Obama (SAFO) a press release, *"highlighting the role of desis in the Iowa caucus,"* said desis *"played an active and important role in canvassing and get-out-the-vote efforts that led to Senator Barack Obama's (D-IL) decisive and historic victory in last night's Democratic presidential caucus in Iowa."* [823] SAFO hosted *"monthly phone banking nights since August,"* and used a college email: *"please have them e-mail saja@columbia.edu."* [823] Note: Columbia Professor Jagdish Bhagwati promoted outsourcing.

Bundling to Get Government Posts & Deals!

"The Top Indian-American Bundlers" a SAJA post claimed: *"Many bundlers secure government posts if their candidate wins, or have the inside track on lucrative business deals."* The list showed Hillary Clinton was in the lead with ten. Obama had six. Romney had two. McCain had one. None were listed for Ron Paul or Mike Huckabee. [824] Did they not get money because they would not give *"government posts"* and *"lucrative business deals"* to bundlers?

"Hillary's Indian Supporters Move to Obama," a SAJA post said Kamil Hasan was *"one of two South Asian super delegates"* who had planned to support Hillary because, *"we have known Senator Clinton and Bill Clinton in the past."* But, things changed in June 2008 when Obama called. Hasan asked about US relations with India. Obama promised *"that it would be one of the most strategic relationships."* Hassan *"told Obama he should consider including Indian Americans in the administration if he is elected president, and Obama told him he would definitely consider it."* Hasan said, *"So based on that, I endorsed him."* [826]

Two months after Obama *agreed not to oppose outsourcing* and to give government posts to South Asians he raised *a record $7.8 million at a San Francisco fundraiser.* *"One-hundred-and fifty Indians and Pakistanis showed up, many of them from the who's who of Silicon Valley."* Couples paid $28,300 to attend the VIP ballroom gala. Kanwal Rekhi who is often referred to as the "godfather" of the India "Mafia," and Nancy Pelosi attended this fundraiser. [805] Kamil Hasan told angry reporters who could not get in: *"It was a private fundraiser and press are not allowed at such events."* [805]

Despite the media block out, the *San Francisco Chronicle* wrote: "Obama Reaps Big Bucks at S.F. Fundraisers," that said *"Obama used his own name and heritage to make a point"* saying he had a *"lifelong association with their cultures,"* and *"an orientation toward Asia."*

Obama told them his Occidental College roommate was Pakistani, and, *"his dorm was where, Indians and Pakistanis came together under one roof...to cause havoc in the university."* [815] Was he in an international student dorm? Obama said his friendships with Pakistanis *"have lasted ... for years, and continue until this day ... I have an enormous personal affection for the people of South Asia."* Obama promised South Asians more immigration and told them, *"you are the future."* He said, *"We are going to win this election. We're going to change the country and we're going to change the world... so keep your stress to a minimum."* [815]

As a result, *"Indian Americans ...emerged as significant backers and fund-raisers for Obama's campaign."* They even formed an *"Asian American Finance Committee for the presidential campaign of Obama."* They praised VP pick Biden: *"The Indian American community's links with Senator Biden go back a long way and he has been a strong supporter of the nuclear deal."* [838]

After the election, a "Top Obama fundraisers Get Posts," in *USA Today* reported that 40% of his fundraisers got key jobs. Bundlers got posts on Obama's Cabinet, advisory boards, ambassadorships, and more. Sample of money raised and posts:

- *Nicole Avant over $500,000–Ambassador to the Bahamas.*
- *Gregory Craig $200K to $500K – White House counsel.*
- *Eric Holder $50K to $100K – Attorney General.* [795]

"Taxpayer Calculator: How Much Will the Transition to Digital Medical Records Cost You?" on *foxnews.com* said that the Obama healthcare plan required hospitals and doctors *"to convert millions of paper patient files to digital records."* It was *expected to cost $27 billion dollars.* "Stimulus" money from our taxes was to cover *$19 billion of the cost.* [894] How much of this money went to foreign workers and foreign outsourcing companies? Was it campaign payback to Obama's bundlers?

Obama Campaign Money Flooded In

Obama's 2008 campaign shattered fundraising records. His campaign carefully crafted the perception that the money came from grassroots Americans. However, multiple sources claimed that foreign money oiled Obama's campaign machinery.

"Obama's Foreign Donors: the Media Averts Its Eyes," by the *American Thinker* asked, *"Jihadis donating to Obama from Gaza? Could there be a bigger story? Foreign donations are illegal, but this story was all that and so much more."* [813] It said two Palestinian brothers donated $33,500. The Obama camp claimed they returned the money, but the brothers said they never got a refund. The Obama camp said they thought GA stood for Georgia, so–*"why did they ship the tee shirts to the correct address in Gaza?"* Overseas donations came from:

- *"France, Virgin Islands, Planegg, Vienna, Hague, Madrid, London, AE, IR Milan, Singapore, Beijing, Switzerland, Toronto, Vancouver, La Creche, Pak Chong, Dublin, Panama, Krabi, Berlin, Geneva, Buenos Aires, Prague, Nagoya, Budapest, Barcelona, Sweden, Taipei, Hong Kong, Rio de Janeiro, Sydney, Zurich, Ragusa, Amsterdam, Hamburg, Uganda, Mumbai, Nagoya, Tunis, Zacatecas, St Croix, ..."* [813]

A "Secret, Foreign Money Floods Into Obama Campaign," *Newsmax.com* article reported Obama received, *"the largest pool of unidentified money that has ever flooded into the U.S. election system."* [812] It said a *"whopping $426.9 million Barack Obama has raised has come from small donors whose names the Obama campaign won't disclose."* Obama received $3.38 million from overseas. Only $201,680 was confirmed to be from overseas US diplomats and military. So $94 out of every $100 of the money was not validated as coming from US citizens. The money came from: *"Abu Dhabi, Addis Ababa, Beijing, Fallujah, Florence, Italy, France ..."* [812]

Accepting Illegal "Contributions?"

"Obama Accepting Untraceable Donations" an article in *The Washington Post* reported Obama accepted untraceable prepaid credit cards that could be used by foreign nationals to make illegal contributions. [877]

Moammar Gadhafi said: *"All the people in the Arab and Islamic world and in Africa applauded this man."* However, *"Though Gadhafi asserted that fundraising from Arab and African nations were "legitimate," the fact is U.S. federal law bans any foreigner from donating to a U.S. election campaign."* [812]

US Election Day Events Celebrated in India?!

Here is a shocker, SAJA had a, "Prez Race: U.S. Election Day Events in India," page. Why would Delhi, Hyderabad, Chennai, Bangalore, Kolkata, and Mumbai hold planned events tracking our election? Events in Delhi were to begin with a "Morning Election Watch" at 7:00 am and continue, *"till we know..."* They had a website at www.democratsindia.org. Their "Schedule of Anxiety" included *"a list of swing state poll closing times in India"*:

Indiana, Georgia and Virginia at 5:30 am
Ohio and West Virginia at 6:00 am
Florida, Pennsylvania, Missouri, New Hampshire, Main at 6:30 am
North Carolina 7:00 am
Minnesota, Wisconsin, Arizona, Colorado, New Mexico 7:30 am
Iowa, Montana, Nevada 8:30 am
North Dakota 9:30 am [830]

On this webpage "Steve" commented, "This is the Empire Strikes Back. In that movie Darth Vader's people got the upper hand. But at the next movie the good guys win. So, yeah it is going to be terrible tomorrow. But in four years we are all going to be talking about President elect Jindal. ...Tomorrow is Rock bottom. ... I believe Obama's star is going to fall quite rapidly.... I believe America has a greater destiny ahead of her *I believe this is all to set the stage for Bobby Jindal* to turn America back in the correct direction." [830] They voted for Obama to "set the stage for Jindal."

Social Media Targeting Young Americans

<u>Yes We Did, An Inside Look at How Social Media Built the Obama Brand</u> was a book written by Rahaf Harfoush about our 2008 election. She was *"a full-time volunteer at Obama Headquarters,"* and claimed: *"We ushered in a new age of <u>multiculturalism</u>, activism, and empowerment."* [782] Who is she? According to a 2006 article on *thestar.com*, Harfoush was born in Syria, and described herself as a *"moderate, educated and tolerant Arab-Canadian."* [783]

Harfoush said, *"MoveOn.Org was founded to petition government officials to censure President Bill Clinton and "move on," instead of impeaching him."* She wrote that *MoveOn.org* was a political "national powerhouse" with over 4 million members. *This Clinton political machine then became the Obama political machine.* [782]

What did MoveOn.org gain by keeping Bill Clinton in office?

"In one of his last acts as President, Bill Clinton passed the American Competitiveness in the Twenty-First Century Act." This act increased the H-1B quota limit to 195,000 per year. So under Clinton the H-1B quota tripled from 65,000 to 195,000 per year. [42]

Harfoush said MoveOn *"fused data mining techniques with online phone banking tools."* Callers, *"no matter where they lived,"* only needed an unconfirmed email address to logon to *my.barackobama.com* *"to join in a calling campaign targeting a specific state."* [782] Callers were racially matched and used scripts to *"better control the conversation."* The calls were recorded. [782] Who has these recordings? Even once Americans started voting, *"The online tool guided callers to the district where their efforts were most needed, giving MoveOn the agility to quickly shift priorities <u>as races unfolded</u> and conditions changed."* Over 50,000 people made a total of over 7 million calls during the campaign. [782]

"Emails from Barack Obama were drafted by Stephen Greer and his team." They sent *"hyper-segmented emails that provided readers with customized messaging."* In other words they used your personal data to craft emails that would persuade you to vote for Obama. [782]

Anyone who criticized Obama was removed *"within minutes."* Moreover, they scoured the internet attacking Obama critics and made *"statements you could never make as an organization—no matter how much you want to."* [782] Did they threaten Americans?

Were our universities used for foreign election tampering? "Students for Barack Obama" already had 62,000 members on Facebook when Obama announced his candidacy. It spread to over 550 colleges. [782] Harfoush told how they attracted college students using music, videos, parties, competitions, and social activities to create a sense of community. They sent notes to increase their *"feelings of ownership."* For example, "Tyler in Ohio" wrote, *"I think that this is my generation's moment. This is our chance to right the wrongs that decades of politics as usual has created. Thank you for supporting Barack, you are doing me and our country proud."* [782] Was campaigning for Obama a *"chance to right the wrongs"*? Not according to, "Barack Obama and Slavery," by Bill Warner on *americanthinker.com.* [799] How were young Americans brainwashed into believing our country's history was so bad? America is not perfect and we are always working to improve. However, they need to take a close look at the countries criticizing our country.

Let's take a look at Syria where Harfoush was born. According to the US Department of State, Syria has a history of human rights violations, torture, and discrimination against the Kurdish minority whose children may not be allowed to attend college. Workers in the country illegally have no legal protection. The Syrian Constitution *"requires that the President be a Muslim."* The government restricts speech and controls radio, television, and most newspapers. [785]

Stop Tracking US Job Losses!

To Obama's credit, in August 2009, he proposed to end offshore tax breaks, *"American companies that create jobs overseas take tax deductions on their expenses when they do not pay any American taxes on their profits."* [790]

On the other hand, a 2010, article in *The Washington Post*, "Obama Administration Plans to Close International Labor Comparisons Office," said Obama's team claimed closing this office would save $2 million. Critics objected to shutting down this office that "tracks globalization's winners and losers," and noted that Obama was *"more trade-oriented than the populist rhetoric of Obama's campaign suggested."* [789]

Muslim, Eboo Patel, Named Faith-Based Advisor

"Obama Adviser: U.S. Ideal Place for Renewal of Islam," *a* WND report said: *"Obama named a Chicago Muslim, Eboo Patel to his Advisory Council on Faith-Based and Neighborhood Partnerships"*, and that Patel *"has close ties to the imam who wants to build a 13–story Islamic cultural center near Ground Zero."* It quoted Patel, *"There is now a critical mass of Muslims in America."* [862] Critical mass for what?

Patel said: *"The bulk of the American Muslim community is very young and overwhelmingly under 40."* Patel has close ties to the Islamic Society of America whose leader said a Muslim prayer at Obama's inauguration, and who attended *"Obama's Ramadan dinner at the White House."* [893] Patel's *"under 40"* comment is significant. Did the vast majority of Muslims in our country come here on *non-immigrant student visas* obtained by signing legal agreements that they would not stay? How many got H-1B visas? How many are here illegally trying to get DREAM Act amnesty?

Mike Huckabee Americans' Choice?

Foreign nations that thought they had things all set up were caught off guard when Mike Huckabee won the 2008 GOP caucus. Huckabee spoke against outsourcing and became a target. They wanted Obama or Hillary or McCain.

New Delhi *ndtv.com* "Mike Huckabee: Profile" gave him "*black marks,*" even though as governor he improved education, cut taxes, and left an $800 million surplus. A side banner asked, "*Will Obama's U-turn on outsourcing help India?*" It said McCain was for "free trade." [835] Were American voters told that Obama did a "*U-turn on outsourcing?*" Outsourcing is not "free trade."

A January 2008 SAJA post wrote: "*The Hindu American Foundation, which has consistently fought to uphold the separation of church and state, expressed deep concern and worry about Presidential candidate Mike Huckabee's call to amend the US Constitution according to "God's standards." ...it is an appeal in 'code words' to a people of a particular faith...Our founding fathers understood the importance of freedom of religion, and it is important to bear in mind their vision of a multicultural and multifaith society.*" [841] Huckabee was referring to *the faith of our founding fathers* whose vision was not "*multiculturalism.*" This Hindu group predicted, "*Mike Huckabee may not stay in the race for long.*" [841] Why were they so sure they could eliminate him?

Hindus have a political party, Bharatiya Janata, in India. After learning "*Obama carries a small "monkey god" for good luck,*"–Hindus *planned to give him a 2 ft tall "idol of Hanuman."* [837] Also, a 2003 article, "Diyas Brighten White House," said the Association of Indians in America (AIA) underline confronted Bush at a fundraiser *and pressured him to allow a Hindu religious celebration in the White House.* It said Karl Rove presided over the Deepavali in the White House where, "*Images of Goddess Lakshmi and Lord Ganesh transformed the room.*" [322] In 2009, Obama hosted a Diwali celebration in the White House and bowed to a Hindu priest. [749]

Republicans Need to Wake Up

Republicans need to wake up. Outsourcing contributions have them sedated like a sleep walker oblivious to reality. The top Indian bundlers favored Democrats 18 to 3 in the 2008 election. They "contribute" to Republicans to maintain favorable outsourcing and visa legislation, like they did to control Bush1 and Bush2. However, they will toss Republicans to the curb if they think a Democrat can win.

"Bundling of Campaign Funds Masks Large Donations." [647] "Obama fund-raiser faces new US fraud allegation," a 2009 *Reuters* report claimed that one of the *top "bundlers" of contributions to Obama's presidential campaign,*" was arrested on charges of bank fraud. This fundraiser was *on the board of the Iranian American Political Action Committee.* [807]

Did that record breaking $745 million Obama's campaign received come with a lot of strings attached? "Lobbyists Enjoy Windfall Despite Pledges to Rein in Special Interest Influence," in April 2010 *Fox News* exposed that, *"half of Obama's recess appointments the prior week had special interest connections."* [839]

If you're like most Americans, the big issues for you in 2008 were our economy, jobs, and amnesty. So, how did we end up with John McCain and Barack Obama? Both lacked management credentials. McCain openly supported outsourcing. Obama hid outsourcing connections worse than McCain's. Obama and McCain supported amnesty. *So both candidates struck out on all three counts important to Americans. We had already lost.*

Who won? Foreign nations who profited from outsourcing, money transfers won. Foreign students and foreign workers who wanted visas won. And, illegal aliens who wanted amnesty won.

Chapter 10

"Coalitions of Minorities"

Divisive & Racist

Then: Proud to be an American

Now: "White Privilege"

One of the most disturbing aspects of the hijacking of our democracy is the brainwashing of young Americans. Remember Harfoush's book <u>Yes We Did</u> told how young American college students were lured with parties and other activities into campaigning for Obama. The carrot used was that to be proud of their country and to "right the wrongs" they had to get Obama elected.

The carrot worked. Young Americans voted 2 to 1 for Obama in 2008. This was the biggest political gulf between young voters and their parents and grandparents ever recorded according to the Pew Research Center. [885] Why? The Obama political machine cog *Organizing for America* recruited "campus captains" to drum up excitement for Obama and register students. Obama held rallies on college campuses.

Young Americans were led to believe that Obama cared about them. However, by the 2010 election many were disillusioned. [885]

Universities Teach "White Privilege"

Generations of Americans sacrificed and invested so that their children could have a better life than they had. John Adams said it well in a letter to his wife Abigail, *"I must study politics and war that my sons may have liberty to study mathematics and philosophy. My sons ought to study mathematics and philosophy, geography, natural history, naval architecture, navigation, commerce and agriculture, in order to give their children a right to study painting, poetry, music, architecture, statuary, tapestry, and porcelain."*

The Obama *"guilt vote"* strategy worked because professors used our colleges to disparage our country. Bill O'Reilly did a 2009 segment, "Is University of Minnesota Planning to Teach 'White Guilt' Class?" and said an *"indoctrination is taking place now all across the United States."* [865]

While our culture encourages critical analysis of our forefathers; foreign born professors have taken this too far. *To gain undue political leverage and enrich themselves they hound our kids with "the wrongs" in our history.* US Professor Jagdish Bhagwati called the United States a "selfish hegemon" in his book "In Defense of Globalization," [259] and in his Council on Foreign Relations Op-Ed "The Selfish Hegemon Must offer a New Deal in Trade." This was inappropriate because: we have generously given aid to his native India for over half a century and we trusted and paid him to teach our children. Did we pay for his MIT education?

"University Sponsors Campaign to Undermine 'White Privilege," an analysis by Campus Reform told how the University of Minnesota in 2012 sponsored a *"racial justice"* ad campaign. The ads featured white people with black graffiti writing scrawled across their faces confessing that it was "unfair" that they were white. They said they got better pay and better jobs because they were white. [1031]

"White Privilege?"

Census data since 2000 shows the number of young non-Hispanic white Americans under age 15 declined in 42 states! [694] Why? Has the H-1B visa program caused a decline in the white birth rate? Has teaching "white guilt" in our schools increased teenage suicides? Sadly, studies report *that the American teenager suicide rate has doubled since the 1950s.* Some mental-health professionals blame the increased teenage suicides on *the harmful effects of layoffs on families for causing teenagers to feel hopeless.* [867]

An analysis of US war causalities from 2003 to 2007 showed that 75% were non-Hispanic whites. [842] It concluded since whites made up 75% of the US population that the death rates were fair to minorities. However, about 87% of Americans over the age of fifty are white. Whites only comprise about 57% of Americans age 20 or younger. So, whites were suffering significantly unfair losses. [843] Are young white Americans signing up disproportionately because they are discriminated against in college admissions, scholarships, and jobs? What ethnic groups are not carrying their fair share? American veterans "suicides are also rising at alarming rates." On average 18 military veterans kill themselves per day. [706] What proportion of these suicides are white?

"Troops' Families Feel Weight of War," in 2009 *USAToday* reported <u>long deployments were tearing families apart</u>. [1056] When parents are deployed to war, they are not there to help with homework or to give advice. Adolescents struggle more with school and depression when their parents are deployed. They have many demands beyond school, *"they take on extra chores at home, look after younger siblings, work jobs ..."* [705] It is our nation's moral responsibility to help these children excel in school, and to support them when their parents are deployed.

Diversity Hiring for Redistribution!

Obama used *"diversity czars to promote racial and gender hiring in federal agencies"* according to a 2010, *Fox News* report, "Financial Overhaul Provision to Promote Diversity Hiring in Federal Agencies Stirs Backlash." There were concerns *"diversity czars"* may channel government money, and contracts to *"minority" businesses.* There were also concerns about too much government influence over operations of Federal banks. [857]

Obama's Military Leadership Diversity Commission called *"for greater diversity in the military's leadership"* to mirror the general population. They complained that 77% of senior US military officers were white. As just mentioned in the current war almost 75% of US causalities were white. To achieve diversity Obama wanted to promote non-soldiers such as programmers, and people from other cultures that speak foreign languages to leadership positions in our military! [901]

Here's a shocking statistic, how many Protestants are on the current Supreme Court? None. *This is where we need to start with job redistribution to "mirror the general population" of the United States.* A 2010, *"Fox News Poll: Most OK With No Protestants on Supreme Court,"* claimed that 70% of Americans don't care if no Protestants are on our Supreme Court. All our current Justices came from just three law schools: Harvard, Yale and Columbia. Do these colleges discriminate against Protestants? [855] The majority of Americans are supposed to not care if they are not represented on our Supreme Court. What is going on?

Obama appointed Sotomayor, despite her *'wise Latino woman better than a white man'* comment. Also consider that *"wise Latino"* judges preside over courts in Latin American countries such as *Mexico, Chile, Brazil, Venezuela, Cuba, Peru, Guatemala ...* Are these countries making reciprocal diversity assignments?

Who's Really Unfairly Privileged in America?

USINPAC came up with its *"Coalitions of Minorities"* strategy in 2002 to gain US political clout and wealth. It worked. By 2007, **immigrants from India were the richest people in America!** They had 200,000 millionaires! [625] The "godfather" of the India "Mafia" in the US, a Pakistani, said *Indians seeking venture capital get preferential treatment, "even over whites."* [333]

Most came here as privileged foreign students at our expense, and then stayed illegally. Globally they outnumber us 5 fold. Yet, US political clout got them favored *"minority"* status?!

By 2010 their median income jumped to $69,470 *almost double* the $38,885 overall! At less than 1% of our *population their kids got 10% of Time's touted "young superstars" list.* [1043] How did they merit such power and wealth? What did they contribute to the founding and building of our nation? Are they almost twice as valuable as other Americans? *Are their kids 10 times smarter than other American children?*

Our children are harmed by professors who teach *"white privilege"* instead of how our ancestors' success and wealth came primarily from hard work, inventing, investing, and merit. Contrast this to a college student in India who told *60 Minutes: "We are lucky enough to be told by people around us that we're good and that we have a bright future, and that gives us a lot of confidence."* [323]

A US professor, James Lain, wrote a book in 2003 that criticized India's revered warrior Shivaji. India not only banned his book–they wanted to arrest him. India's Prime Minister Atal Behari Vajpayee declared, *"We not only condemn it, but also warn the foreign author not to play with our national pride..."* [356] Indians should take pride in their county and their heroes; *just as we should take pride in our country and heroes.*

India Abroad Eyes US Presidency

As mentioned earlier *India Abroad* set up the "Indian American Center for Political Awareness" (IACPA) that lobbied Congress to increase H-1B caps, and to grant *illegal aliens "a temporary protected status."*

IACPA's goals: *"to make America not only tolerate diversity, but to value it as a source of American strength... IACPA envisions a world where all children can believe that they can grow up to become President of the United States."* [425]

So *India Abroad* has its eyes on our Presidency. They want a US president with origins from India, and that still identifies with India. How diverse is IACPA and the government of India? Can all children grow up to become Prime Minister of India?

IACPA lobbied for US hate crime legislation that would elevate *"crimes based on race, color, or religion or national origin to Federal offenses."* [425] Yet, it wrote *"Beijing ready to help New Delhi Crush Maoists: Envoy."* [425] That does not sound tolerant.

Ironically, nations criticizing us often have worse histories on immigration, discrimination, and religious persecution. They brainwash and misguide our youth like an out-of-whack compass pointing our kids in the wrong direction.

They use our schools and text books to criticize our country. Yet they try to cover-up the "wrongs" in their countries. For example, a January 2006, article "India History Spat Hits US," Hindus were demanding major changes in US textbooks. Some scholars were alarmed at demands to deny a history of discrimination against women, and to claim the caste system was based on people's capacities. [514]

Look Who's Criticizing US

Americans may find it inappropriate for IACPA to judge our country on equality, tolerance, and *"a guarantee of social acceptance."* Look what India had done in just the past 8 years:

- *India arrests foreign students who overstay according to a 2008 article, "Hyderabad Police Arrest 25 Foreign Students for Overstaying." Ethiopians, Somalians and Djiboutian students were arrested.* [716] *Were arrests based on race and national origin?*

- *Doctors in India held a strike in 2006 to protest affirmative action that would let lower caste Indians (80% of India's population) have 49.5% of government hospital jobs.* [581]

- *"Woman, Baby Die after Doctors Refuse to Treat Them in India," reported in 2008 that she was an "untouchable" and "high-class Hindus fear coming into contact with them." So doctors "refused to touch her or provide medical care as she delivered her baby."* [692]

- *In 2008, it was reported that in India "dozens of women are killed every year on suspicion of being witches or witch doctors."* [717]

- *"As India's Wealth Rises, A Woman's Limited Dowry Could Mean Her Death," a 2007 article claimed "a woman was killed over dowry every 77 minutes." The women were: "beaten to death, burned alive, electrocuted, poisoned, pushed out windows or otherwise killed horrifically."* [701]

- *According to a 2005 article, Hindus burned 92 Muslims to death in riots, and 3,200 had been arrested as suspects in "more than 300 cases of violence against Muslims."* [610]

- *"Hindu Extremists' Reward to Kill Christians, as Britain Refuses to Bar Members" a 2008 TimesOnline story reported 67 Christians were murdered, thousands had their homes destroyed, and 11,000 Christians were living in fear as refugees.* [781]

- *A people's rights advocate Kailash Satyarthi was working to abolish slave-camps in India in 2005, according to PBS.* [426]

Positioning Piyush "Bobby" Jindal For Presidency

Recall that *India Abroad* was eyeing our presidency. A 2008 blog said McCain's veep should be Jindal– *"What better way to show that the GOP is by far the party of "inclusiveness" than to <u>nominate a rising star from India descent</u>"* [698] As Commander-in-Chief of our military?

It is troubling that when Jindal was a US Congressman he was named *"India Abroad Person of the Year in 2005."* [697] That year he cosponsored *House Resolution 227* lobbied for by USINPAC. India wanted the bill to help promote "Brand IIT" globally to compete against the US. [342] Was Jindal selected because of this resolution; or, because of his previous job with *McKinsey & Co. a consulting firm that advised American corporations to hire H-1Bs, and outsource our jobs to India.* [697]

With support from *USINPAC* Jindal, became the Governor of Louisiana in 2008. [993] He was the *first governor of India ancestry and the youngest in US history.* [697] [904] "<u>Now, the Real Test for Bobby Jindal</u>" a *hindu.com* article, said Hindus should dance in the streets because Jindal, "<u>*someone who looks like us*</u>," won the Louisiana governor race. Yet, Hindus complained *"about his silence on racism...Jindal voted against hate crimes legislation and for strict immigration enforcement."* [904]

It would be absurd for Jindal, a millionaire governor whose parents came here on a student visa, to complain of US racism. It appears more likely that he received preferential treatment.

Hindus want US hate crime laws? "Christians Face Hindus' Wrath" a 2008 story in *The Washington Post* reported Hindus looted Christian villages, *burned Bibles*, and chanted: *"India is for Hindus! ...Christianity is a foreign religion."* The story said "<u>*an Australian missionary and his two sons were burned alive*</u>" in 1999! [905] What happened to tolerance?

Jindal got the plum media spot as Republican spokesman after the 2008 election. He compared his parents to Obama's father, and called Obama's election a *"redemptive journey."* What's to redeem? Obama's father was a privileged foreign student educated at our expense. Jindal feigned empathy for Americans who lost their jobs. His outsourcing connections make this hard to swallow. His speech was "widely-panned."

Despite his poor performance, Jindal was soon back in the spotlight. Morley Safer in a *60 Minutes* segment deified Jindal as *"the grand old party's savior,"* and said Jindal's *"name was raised repeatedly as a potential running mate for John McCain."* He proclaimed Jindal as the *"first non-white governor of Louisiana since reconstruction"* and disdained *"lily-white, good ol' boys."* [751] It is racist to infer that non-white candidates are preferable and less corrupt. Had Safer done his homework, he would have known political corruption in India makes those *"lily-white, good ol' boys"* look like a minor league.

"In Criticizing cleanup, Jindal Finds His Voice," a 2010, *Wall Street Journal* story said, *"Mr. Jindal's aggressive stance ... puts the 38-year-old governor back on the national stage."* [787] Another 2010 article, "Indian-Americans Gaining Clout in US Politics," said they were *pleased Obama gave them so many appointments* including the only *"father-son"* appointees. Because they fund candidates *"who look like me,"* they had *"growing influence."* [1043] How can they back candidates based on race, and then complain about racism?

In 2012 Senator Vitter was warned his *"birthright citizenship"* bill could harm Jindal. He replied, *"The anchor baby rule clearly acts as a magnet to draw more illegal immigrant parents here. If we don't solve that and the illegal immigration problem, it won't much matter who's running for president."* [907]

Slavery–Everything is Not Black and White

Our universities welcome "white privilege" speakers such as Katrina Brown whose *"ancestors were the largest slave-trading family in US history."* She unfairly ascribes the guilt to *"white Americans more broadly."* [866] Her history is not the history of most white Americans.

It is unjust to racially profile and blame all white people for slavery. Only 1.4% of US citizens owned slaves at the start of the Civil War. A far greater percentage of white Americans risked their lives fighting to free slaves, and some helped slaves escape through the Underground Railroad. Besides, some free blacks and Native Americans owned slaves. [614] White people did not start the black slave trade. The black slave trade began when African kings sold prisoners from tribal wars:

- *"The king said that he was ready to do anything ... except to give up the slave trade... The slave trade has been the ruling principle of my people. It is the source of their glory and wealth. Their songs celebrate their victories and the mother lulls the child to sleep with notes of triumph over an enemy reduced to slavery."* [668]

- *Also there are books such as: John Azumah's book about slavery, "The Legacy of Arab-Islam in Africa."* [884]

Another "guilt" ploy is to claim our nation's wealth came from slavery–if this was the case then the West Indies and Brazil would each be 8 to 9 times as wealthy as the US based on the number of slaves bought. [668] Our greatest achievements came after slavery was abolished.

White people were also the victims of slavery. Vikings raided Europe taking English, Irish, and Scottish slaves from 700's -1000's. The invasions of Europe continued, with Barbary pirates taking a million or more European slaves from the 16th through the 19th centuries.

Books Altered to be Anti-European

Many books have been rewritten with an anti-European viewpoint. For example, the *Collins Atlas of World History* first published in 1978 was radically altered in 2003. The Introduction said earlier releases had a "Eurocentric" view which was *"misleading and untenable."* It said Europeans only wrote about other countries when Europeans *"impinged upon them."* [382]

Later on the atlas acknowledged foreign invaders raided and killed vast numbers of Europeans. And, the Black Death plague that originated in Asia killed 25 million Europeans. [382] So who "impinged" on who?

The atlas states that in comparison to Islam, Europeans were backward and did not catch up to other world civilizations until the 15th century. Even then it said Ottoman Turks accomplishments "overshadowed" the backward Europeans. [382]

It is cruel and untrue to teach white children that their ancestors lagged behind other races. A 1998 PBS segment, "Mysterious Mummies of China" reported remarkable mummies were found in the Takla Makan Desert–buried 1,000 years before the first East Asian people arrived. The report claimed the *"mummy people shaped the very future of civilization"* when they established the Great Silk Road. Paintings in nearby caves showed they had blond or red hair, and bluish-green eyes. A painting of a blond person with a tiki caste mark indicated they also had contact with people from India. [385]

In 2005, genetic testing revealed that the mummy people had Caucasoid/Europoid genes–i.e. they were genetically the same as Europeans. The artifacts and clothes discovered proved that the ancient ancestors of Europeans were an advanced civilization. They used the wheel, and wore fine woolen textiles that are the oldest wool clothes ever found. [384]

Black Panther Voter Intimidation Case Dropped

"Charges Against 'New Black Panthers' Dropped by Obama Justice Dept." *Fox News* reported a poll watcher with civil rights experience said *"it was the most blatant form of voter intimidation he had ever seen."* [806] "Justice at the Justice Department?" reported several DOJ employees said *they were told voting rights laws do not protect whites.* Congressman Frank Wolf said the DOJ was "stonewalling" a congressional probe. Commissioner Todd Gaziano, said the Black Panther case was, *"a scandal of epic proportions...The only evidence we have from live witnesses is that this case was dismissed because of hostility to race-neutral enforcement of the civil rights law."* [900]

Amnesty to "Create a Governing Coalition!"

"Obama Adviser: Amnesty to Ensure 'Progressive' Rule," a 2010 WND article quoted Eliseo Medina VP of the Service Employees International Union (SEIU): *"We reform the immigration laws, it puts 12 million people on the path to citizenship and eventually voters... We will be creating a governing coalition for the long term, not just for an election cycle."* [847] This sounds like a foreign plot to use amnesty as a weapon to takeover our nation. According to the article, *"SEIU is closely linked to the controversial"* ACORN. [847]

"Yo Decido. Why Latinos will pick the next President," was the title of the March 5, 2012 issue of *Time.* [995] Why is our media racially divisive? Anyone with common sense could see this title marginalized other Americans as if their votes do not matter. *Such inflammatory statements may cause US citizens to oppose not only amnesty but any further immigration.* "A Republican Probably Can't Win Without About 40 percent, Minimum, of the Hispanic and Latino Vote," an *American Voice* lobby article claimed in 2012 that 84% want DREAM Act amnesty. [984] Amnesty will weaken, not strengthen Republicans.

It is Time to End "Coalitions of Minorities"

It is time to remind our politicians this is a country of Americans, by Americans, for Americans. We are proud of our heritage and proud to be Americans. Ronald Reagan said, *"What I'd really like to do is go down in history as the President who made Americans believe in themselves again."*

Most Americans welcome immigrants of other races who come here to adopt our culture and are not racially divisive. However, using amnesty and visa fraud to drastically change the demographics of our country, and then to seize ethnic political power to benefit a foreign nation is un-American.

It is unacceptable for immigrants, who swear allegiance to the United States of America, to turn and attack our national heritage and our heroes. The "Coalitions of Minorities" political strategy is racist and destructive.

Teaching *"white privilege"* in our schools must stop. Foreign nations are brainwashing whites to feel guilty, and blacks to hate whites and to feel inadequate. It's the old game of *"Let's you and him fight"* so that they can take advantage of both using H-1B visas and offshoring. Ironically, black Americans are being manipulated by a network that took minority benefits that should have gone to them.

It is not right to racially profile white people, and then turn around and forbid racial profiling of other ethnic groups. Our founding fathers were white. Children suffer when their ancestors and our nation's history are disparaged. Schools need to teach that while our forefathers and nation are not perfect, on the world stage they are among the best. We owe our founding fathers esteem and recognition. They earned it.

Many Immigrants Embrace American Culture

Not all professors from India promoted outsourcing. For example, college professors Ron and Anil Hira wrote the book *Outsourcing America* which called outsourcing "Fool's Gold for Companies." They poked holes in contrived outsourcing "studies" used to sell outsourcing. [888] Moreover, Ron Hira warned offshoring could cost our technology leadership. [129] Dinesh D'Sousa, wrote a book *What's So Great About America*. He explained that our enemies hate America because it stands for freedom. He pointed out that most nations had slavery. America was unique because we fought a civil war to abolish slavery. [270]

Dispossession Redistribution Needs to Stop

Obama's "Diversity Czar" scheme is un-American and dangerous. Leadership in our military needs to be earned not handed out–especially not to people who gained citizenship through visa fraud or amnesty.

If Obama wants work and educational opportunities to *"mirror the general population,"* our military where 75% of the population gets 77 out of every 100 jobs is the wrong place to start. The biggest problem is in our grad schools where ethnic groups that make up 1-3% of our population are taking 50-70 out of every 100 seats. Next, jobs as university professors and physicians where 1-3% of our population takes 20-35 of every 100 jobs. Next should be programming jobs, accounting jobs, and other professional jobs.

Chapter 11

US Election Fraud

Tentacles of election fraud slithered in from multiple directions.

There were several reports of voter fraud in 2008 and 2012. When someone votes illegally, they do not just vote for a presidential candidate. They have a full ballot. They vote for Senators, Representatives, State and local politicians, and even judges.

Our nation was ripe for foreign tampering because we had millions of foreign students, foreign workers and illegal aliens in our country whose status was dependent on visas and amnesty. Not only did they have insider access to our computers in many cases our voting machines were programmed by non-citizens!

How could a foreign nation pull off millions of illegal votes? It would need access to our computers storing voter lists, and computers storing the names and addresses of citizens who had died, or moved, or did not plan to vote. A computer program could be written that create a list of Americans who are on a state's voter list; and, on a list of people who had died, or moved, or did not plan to vote. On Election Day if a state's voting wasn't going how they wanted, they could easily use phone banks to call people in an area and give them a name and address on the voting list they could use to steal an Americans identity to go get a ballot, and then illegally vote.

Obama Deceived Voters on Offshoring

On the Charlie Rose Show in 2009 Jagdish Bhagwati, the economics professor who criticized John Kerry for opposing outsourcing and called offshoring our jobs "free trade," debated Senator Sherrod Brown who was concerned about our overseas job losses. [849] Bhagwati made an unsettling revelation: *"Very clearly the president believes in the virtues of free trade. He's always been giving that away. I think like any democratic candidate, he had to be saying things against trade somewhere to get elected."* [849]

Obama used our media to mislead us. Only outsourcing benefactors knew the truth.

Voting Machine Election Fraud?

Recall our government was warned that electronic voting was vulnerable to tampering. A "Phantom Obama Vote Appears on NJ voting Machine," article asked, *"why doesn't the number on the tapes that indicates the total number of votes cast for candidates match the number on the tapes that indicates the voter turnout?"* [818] When election officials wanted two independent experts to examine the machines, *"Sequoia intervened and threatened a lawsuit if officials allowed the academics to touch the machines."* However, a judge ruled that the experts could test the software and machines, based on a case *"which argues that touch-screen voting machines that don't produce a paper trail are illegal and unconstitutional in New Jersey."* [818]

"Election Software Company Could Intercept and Change Ballots Without a Trace," an October 2012 article warned that military and other overseas voting was vulnerable to tampering. *"Intercepting and changing these ballots, as well as voting electronically on behalf of service people that have no idea such a thing is happening"* could be done by a company tallying votes. [2048] Does this explain the *92% drop in Virginia military absentee ballot requests* and other declines? [1049] *Were our troops concerned their votes may be altered?*

Cover-ups of Felony Illegal Voting!?

It is a felony for a non-citizen to vote in a US election. Yet there may be millions of non-citizens registered to vote. For example, the Colorado Secretary of State, Scott Gessler, reported his department *uncovered almost 12,000 non-citizens who were registered to vote in Colorado.* He testified to the Administrations' Elections subcommittee, *"We know we have a problem here. We don't know the size of it."* He wanted people to provide written proof of citizenship. However Charles Gonzalez (D-Texas) protested saying they did not have "precise numbers." [892]

Each illegal vote cast negates a US citizen's legal vote denying citizens their right to be counted.

"Immigrant Who Voted Illegally on Road to Becoming a US Citizen," was a 2010 *Fox News* story. Debbie Steidl, County Administrator of Elections in Putnam County Tennessee was given a Homeland Security "form letter" by a foreigner who had illegally registered to vote in 2004 and then voted. The DHS told the man how to get his name removed from the voter roll to destroy evidence he illegally voted. Steidl said, *"this frightens me for my country...Why would you let someone who committed voter fraud become a citizen? ...He signed a piece of paper that said he was a citizen of the U.S., just so he could vote. What else could he be willing to do?"* [882] Note a *"form letter"* would indicate DHS was helping a large number of foreigners who illegally voted destroy evidence of felony crimes.

"Obama Justice Department Shut down ACORN probe: FBI documents 'reflect systematic voter registration fraud'" by WND reported they were registering children, felons, non-citizens, and some people multiple times. The Obama Justice Department claimed ACORN had broken no laws." [809] However, in 2010 Fox News reported: "Former ACORN workers Have Been Convicted or Admitted Guilt in Election Fraud." [883]

Voting Fraud?

A report on *thesteadydrip.blogspot.com*, "Obama: More Evidence for Election Fraud Charges," claimed that "*3 Million registered voters are dead, 12 million more ineligible, and 98% of them voted for Obama.*" It said a study found that people who died and people who had moved were still on voter registration rolls. [810]

WND also ran an article titled, "Electoral College Scam: Where Dead People Vote." Bob Unruh reported that Chris Myers, the director of research for the California Democratic Party, said there were errors in the list of eligible voters. [848]

Shortly after the 2008 election TwoCircles.net featured a top banner that pictured Obama and read "*Get the Grants That you Voted For, Click Here.*" The left side banner displayed Obama memorabilia for sale. The page was titled, "Obama raised record $745 million in presidential campaign." There is a problem however, TwoCircles website "About Us" states, "*I belong to two circles of equal size, but which are not concentric. One is India, and the other is the Muslim world.*" [811] This website was for India's Muslim community. It's illegal for them to vote in our election. How many Muslims from India got student grants under Obama?

"Did Illegal Aliens Steal the Election for Obama?" was a 2012 WND story. [1045] "The Big List of Vote Fraud Reports," another WND article compiled a summary of many reports of fraud during our 2012 election. [1046]

"22 Signs That Voter Fraud is Wildly Out of Control And the Election Was a Sham," was a November 2012 report that contained a comprehensive list of fraud including *people showing up to vote who were told they already voted!* [1047]

"Stunned" by Election Fraud

Catherine Engelbrecht, a US citizen, along with a group of her friends, volunteered to help in the 2008 election at polling places in Houston, Texas. They were stunned by what they saw: *"It was fraud, and we watched like deer in the headlights."* [880] As a result, they formed a citizens' group to investigate voter fraud.

They decided to look for houses with more than six registered voters, seeing this as a red flag. Digging through mountains of data, they hit pay dirt when they found a Democratic district with 24,000 houses that had six or more registered voters per house. They spent *"tens of thousands of hours"* following the tracks of voting fraud. Several trails lead to vacant lots with registered voters. One trail led to an eight bed halfway house that had 40 registered voters. [880]

Mentally Disabled Victims of Voter Fraud?

Census figures show we have 16 million Americans with limited mental abilities. A *Fox News* story, "Family of Minnesota Man with Mental Disabilities Says He is a Victim of Voter Fraud" reported Alan Stene claimed his mentally disabled son and other residents of a group home were taken to vote in 2010. He said his son "did not have a clue" of who he voted for. His son said a worker from the home *"just told me who to vote for."* [891] There were similar complaints in 2012 by other families.

This is a sensitive issue. However, we require people to pass a test to get a driver's license. Before the next election this vulnerability in our voting process needs to be addressed in a kind and just way. Otherwise, election tampering could exploit the mentally disabled to manipulate up to 16 million votes.

Were Candidates Properly Vetted?

Our founding fathers required that the president be "natural born" to assure the president would grow up and bond with Americans and have no divided loyalties. McCain was vetted even though he, his father, and grandfather served distinguished military careers in service to our country. Yet, Obama was not properly vetted. Obama spent his early bonding years going to school in a foreign country. Therefore, his associates, papers, and records should have been carefully reviewed to determine his loyalties. Both Obama's father and his stepfather were foreign Muslims. Obama's book <u>Dreams from My Father</u> shows he identifies with his non-American father.

The church Obama attended preached hatred of America.

Recall Obama in a private fundraiser told South Asians that his *friendships with Pakistanis "have lasted ... for years, and continue until this day ... I have an enormous personal affection for the people of South Asia."* [815] Contrast this, to Obama as Commander-in-Chief who was cold and detached when he gave a "shout out" before mentioning the Fort Hood massacre. Something is not right.

We Need to Ensure Our Elections are Valid

Our right to vote is a precious family heirloom passed down from generation to generation. We know it was purchased at a great cost. It is a priceless treasure that we must guard.

We have an infestation of foreign tampering with our elections. It spreads destruction and is hidden in the halls of our government like termites that invade houses. On the surface the structure may still look sound; however, on closer examination it is being secretly eaten away. We need to clean out the infestation and make repairs putting our house in order to make sure the integrity of our elections is restored.

Chapter 12

2012 Election What

Happened?

Accelerating into economic disaster.

Whathappened during our 2012 election? Once again the mainstream media "tipped the scales in favor of Obama." Keep in mind that Soros, a Saudi Prince, and multi-national corporations owned extensive media shares. They had the clout to influence election coverage. Media put out a positive spin even when Obama had to bus in people for the convention and had low attendance at rallies.

Fox News listed *"Five Ways the Mainstream Media,"* tilted coverage in Obama's favor: [1052]

1) *Biased gaffe control covered up Obama gaffes*
2) *Fact-checkers called "accurate statements" lies*
3) *Biased debate monitors*
4) *Benghazi blackout*
5) *Burying the bad economy* [1052]

"Drop in Jobless Figure Gives Jolt to Race for President," an October news report said Obama's campaign was bolstered by a favorable jobs report. The good news– we were just 61,000 shy of having *"nearly the same number of jobs as when Mr. Obama took office."* [1052] Media represented this as a good jobs report?

Town Hall 2012 Closer Look

Let's look at key revelations made in the Town Hall debate that were glanced over by the media. Obama claimed to be an advocate for *"middle class folks"* and young American college graduates. And, that he added 5.2 million new jobs. [1053]

Obama pointed out that Romney *"invested in companies that were pioneers of outsourcing to China, and is currently investing in other countries."* He told Romney, *"You're the last person who's going to get tough on China."* Romney acknowledged that his investments were managed by a *"blind trust, And I understand they do include investments outside the United States, including in –in Chinese Companies."*

Then Romney turned-the-tables and told Obama: *"Let me give you some advice. Look at your pension. You also have investments in Chinese companies. You also have investments outside the United States. You also have investments through a Cayman's trust."* [1053] Are federal pensions invested in foreign countries!? Maybe we need laws that require our politicians and especially our president cannot have foreign investments while in office.

Regarding visas and green cards Romney largely agreed with Obama: *"I also think that we should give visas to people-green cards, rather, to people who graduate with skilled that we need. People around the world with accredited degrees in science and math get a green card stapled to their diploma, to come to the U.S. of A."* [1053] So if China and India graduate a million students a year they would all automatically get green cards to work in our country and compete with Americans for jobs?

This shows that after the primaries were over, *middle class Americans had already lost the election.* No wonder George Soros said that there was "Not Much Difference" between Obama and Romney! [1060]

What the Media Should Have Told You

The media should have told you that the number of jobs added while Obama has been in power is canceled out by the number of jobs lost. *There were no net job gains.*

Obama also conveniently did not mention how many foreign work permits he granted. For example, in January 2012 *NumbersUSA* wrote, *"Obama Speech Brags About 3 Million New Jobs (Fails to Mention 3 Million New Foreign Work Permits)."* [1054]

Obama was channeling US jobs to foreign workers not *middle class folks and young American college graduates!*

- ■   *In 2010 Obama appointees "bullied" US Citizenship and Immigration Services "career staff into <u>rubberstamping approvals for green cards</u> and benefits."* [1055]

- ■   *In 2012, The Daily Exclusive: Rubber Stamp," reported US Citizenship and Immigration Services management was "Pressuring rank-and-file officers to <u>rubber-stamp immigrants' visa applications</u>....One-quarter of the 254 officers surveyed said they have been pressured" into approving cases even when they had "concerns <u>about fraud, eligibility or security.</u>"* [976]

- ■   *January 2012, The New York Times, "Easier Route to Green Card to be Proposed for Some," reported, "<u>President Obama supports (legislation) that would give legal status to **millions of illegal immigrants**</u>" and Obama was "looking for ways to help immigrant communities <u>without going through the partisan dissention in Congress.</u>"* [979]

Obama took a bad economic situation created by Bush-Clinton-Bush and made it much worse. We had high unemployment and no need for more foreign workers.

Logically, if there were *no net job gains,* and Obama *channeled millions of US jobs to foreign workers,* then <u>*Obama caused millions of Americans to lose their jobs!*</u>

The fact that Americans were losing jobs in record numbers is substantiated by home foreclosures. Almost two million American homes were in foreclosure each year he has been in office. [1039] That's about 8 million homes. *If on average two children lived in each home that would be 16 million innocent American children traumatized by home foreclosures!* Where was the media coverage?

Obama had the audacity to claim he was the choice to: "*Make sure your kids can go to college. Make sure that you're a getting a good paying job, making sure that Medicare and Social Security...*" If you are a young college age American, Obama hurt you the most. If your parents lost jobs how could you afford college? Obama increased foreign student visas! And in turn, *your college tuition costs jumped 25% which means college cost almost as much as buying a house. And, your unfair burden of our national debt jumped to $218,676!* [1059] [1061] *Moreover, H-1Bs take mostly entry level jobs that should have gone to you and your friends.*

The media should have told you it wasn't just Obama. November 29, 2011, with bipartisan support the House passed bill HR 3012 to repeal the 7% per country limits on green cards for visa workers such as H-1Bs. India and China lobbied for this bill sponsored by:

- *Jason Chaffetz (R, UT), and cosponsored by 5 Republicans: Jeff Flake (AZ), Robert Goodlatte (VA), Tim Griffin (AR) Lamar Smith (TX), Glenn Thompson (PA): and by 6 Democrats: Luis Gutierrez (IL), Rush Holt (NJ), Jesse Jackson Jr. (IL), Zoe Lofgren (CA), Carolyn Maloney (NY), James Moran Jr. (VA).* [974]

In January 2012 this bill granting millions of green cards still had to pass the Senate. It was being held by Senator Grassley who was standing up for Americans.

Millions of Green Cards Threaten Your Future

Recall India's NDTV posted a YouTube video, "President Obama's Team India?" January 2012, NDTV posted *The New York Times* green card story and wrote: "Long Wait for Green Cards Could Soon Be Over" for "highly skilled immigrants" (i.e. H-1Bs) to become permanent US residents. The backlog of applicants from *India so far exceeded legal limits it would take 70 years to get this many*. NDTV explained that Gutierrez got onboard with the bill because it would also *double green cards for Mexicans and Filipinos* for family chain immigration. [979]

This New Delhi news claimed, "*The Immigrants and their employers have passed labor market tests showing that qualified Americans were not available for the jobs*." [979] Really?

Why don't we require all these millions of jobs be posted to let Americans apply, and make sure they are not unfairly screened out?

Granting millions of green cards makes these foreigners permanent residents eligible to:

- *Collect social security when they retire. This legislation could cause our already overextended social security program to fail.*

- *Sponsor family members for green cards.*

- *Make Political Contributions, even though they can't legally vote.*

- *Receive in-state tuition and the right to apply for taxpayer funded financial aid for education.*

- *Security clearances and enter and leave the US at will.*

- *Form startup companies (to channel in more visa workers); get grants & exemptions from export restrictions.* [981]

American Voice, a pro-amnesty pro-DREAM Act lobby, also reported about Obama green cards: "Obama Administration Announces New Family Unity Waivers." [984]

USINPAC Database Profiles Our Candidates

USINPAC's 2012 election mantra was to claim India did not cause US job losses, but rather that we had a huge shortage of programmers. [921] It *compiled a big brother like database that tracked our politicians' compliance with its agenda such as the* US-India Nuclear Deal, *"position on pro family (chain migration) & pro business (H-1B) visas," trips to India, and much more.* USINPAC's database included photos, personal details such as:

- *Rep. John Boehner (R-OH) was rated 33%. (They recorded no trip to India and no Indian-American on his staff, but he got points because he–Voted* Yes on US-India Nuclear Deal *.)*
  - *Born November 17, 1949, in Cincinnati, Ohio.*
  - *Religion Roman Catholic.*
  - *BS in Business from Xavier University, 1977*
  - *Elected in 2006, got 136,863 votes, raised $2,399,951 (43% individuals & 53% PACs)* [922]

- *Sen. Richard Durbin (D-IL) was rated 55% (He made a trip to India. He doesn't have an Indian-American on his staff but ranked higher because he's a "Contact Lawmaker" who sponsored the "DREAM Act," plus he–Voted* Yes on US-India Nuclear Deal.*)*
  - *Born November 21, 1944 in East Saint Louis, IL*
  - *Religion Roman Catholic*
  - *JD, Georgetown University, 1966*
  - *Elected in 2002, got 2,103,766 votes. Raised $6,250,611 (74% individuals & 20% PACs)*

- *Rep. Michelle Bachman (R-MN)* Voted No on US-India Nuclear Deal, *and is an evangelical. She was not given a rating apparently they wanted her eliminated from the 2012 race.*

The "US-India nuke deal wins support from key Congressman" was a post on *indianmuslims.info*. It claimed USINPAC was *"one of several Indian-American political groups that are working on the issue. ...A fast-growing, affluent and well-educated group of Indian Americans has launched an intensive drive to win support for the deal in the US Congress with lobbying, campaign contributions and public relations."* [939]

Obama's Database Profiles You to Win Election

"Obama's Data Advantage," a June 2012 Politico report said, *"more than 150 techies are quietly peeling back the layers of your life. They know what you read, where you shop, what kind of work you do and who you count as friends. They also **know who your mother voted for in the last election**."* [1062] Is this legal?

But that is not all, *"by harnessing the growing power of Facebook and other online sources, the campaign is building what some see as an unprecedented data base to develop highly specific profiles of potential voters. This allows the campaign to tailor messages directly to them..."* [1062]

In other words they invade your privacy and once they profile you, then they tell you what you want to hear. This is manipulating voters. The campaign message should be honest and open to the public so that we all hear the same message.

The article said: "***Obama campaign official guards details about its digital operation as fiercely as Romney guards his tax returns***." Most of what they were doing was kept secret. They hired *"nonpolitical tech innovators, software engineers and statisticians."* [1062] Were any of these people gathering personal information on Americans foreign students or programmers?

An Obama campaign advisor said *"Facebook was just a site to see friends four years ago now it is part of people's DNA."* According to the article, *"Obama invites supporters to long on to the campaign through their Facebook accounts, which gives the campaign one more avenue for data."* [1062] So if you have a Facebook friend who volunteers to help Obama guess what?

The article said Obama has 27 million *Facebook* followers and 16 million *Twitter* followers. And commented that it was hard to tell ***how many were "non-American*."**

Guess Who Knows How You Voted in 2012

Privacy of your voting is essential to freedom.

However, "*If you voted this election season, President Obama almost certainly has a file on you. His vast campaign database included information on voters' magazine subscriptions, car registrations, housing values and hunting licenses, along with scores estimating how likely they were to cast ballots for his reelection*," according to a *washingtonpost.com* report on "The Obama's Voter Database." [1063]

Imagine serving in our military under a Commander-in-Chief who knows you didn't vote for him/her. A President has the power to send you on life threatening assignments, or to cut your job.

Imagine being a hardworking successful business owner and you have a President who knows you didn't vote for him/her. A president can channel millions of dollars to your competitors and put you out of business. A president can burden you with regulations and taxes that cripple your business.

Imagine you are a private citizen who made a negative comment on Facebook about a politician. Later, you discover that because a Facebook friend linked to a campaign site—your private comment is now stored in a computer database.

Imagine that all your personal data and data on your children reside in a big brother database tracking you.

Other Democrats want to use "Obama's Database" to help them win elections. [1063]

Of course, Obama did not design nor create this database—he's not a programmer. Did foreign professors, foreign students or foreign workers who want amnesty propose and develop this database? Are non-citizens and foreign governments able to access this database?

College Professors and Staff Bias

Where is the diversity in our universities?

Campus Reform a student advocacy group found that, "<u>96% of Ivy League Professors' Donations Went to Obama</u>." [1030] Campus Reform spokesperson Josiah Ryan said, *"These numbers represent more evidence that grand claims of diversity and tolerance on the American campus ring hollow. It is <u>impossible to believe that professors did not protect their financial investment in President Obama through Campaigning in the classroom</u>."* [1030]

"Four of the top ten organizations whose staff donated to President Obama's reelection campaign were universities," according to the Federal Election Commission. Staff of The University of California was the largest donor giving $1,092,906. The list also included Harvard, Stanford, and Columbia. [1050] How much grant money did these universities receive for foreign students? Do the demographics of the faculty, staff and students in our Ivy League colleges mirror our population? Or, do they discriminate against WASPs?

Not one university was a top donor to Republicans.

American College Grads Need Jobs & Insurance

Had Obama cut green cards, H-1Bs and other foreign worker visas at the beginning of his 1ˢᵗ term our economy would be well on its way to a strong recovery (See the book <u>False Prophets of False Profits</u>.) *NumbersUSA's* "Recent College Grads Suffering in Job Market as Pres. Obama Asks for More Foreign Workers in Their Fields," found: *"Only 53% of Americans who graduated from college between 2006 and 2010 have full time jobs."* And, 40% of the ones working are underemployed in jobs that do not require their degree. Starting salaries dropped 10%, while college debt soared. [991] Obama is denying young Americans your American Dream.

Huckabee was in the Lead Again?

People controlling our media, and foreign nations economically exploiting America obviously do not want Mike Huckabee to be our President.

A *USA Today* Gallup Poll in December 2009 showed Huckabee in the lead again. But the media was determined to eliminate him from the race before it even began. "*Mike Huckabee: Stumbling Before race Started*," a news report said after the poll was taken, Maurice Clemmons killed four police officers and since *Huckabee commuted his sentence (9 years earlier)* it "undercuts" his claim of "being an effective governor." [834] Really?

Where is the media coverage of:

- *The "stumbling" politicians whose excessive and lax visa legislation allowed the 9/11 terrorists into our country who killed many police and firefighters and thousands of Americans?*

- *The "stumbling" politicians who allowed illegal aliens free to roam in our country taking jobs Americans need, and many of whom are in prison for crimes harming and killing Americans?*

- *What about all the "stumbling" politicians who passed H-1B visa legislation without verifying the worker shortages, and caused millions of highly educated Americans to lose the jobs they needed to provide for their families?*

Our voices are being drummed out by outsourcing political "contributions" benefiting foreign nations. It is time to take a stand and hold politicians to their oath to represent the American people. Politicians who received a lot of money need to be monitored to make sure they do not abuse their position to financially reward bundlers or other 'contributors.' If they act like they are bought and paid for, then we need to remove them from office.

Shore Up Election Integrity

It is very disconcerting that Obama opposed voter IDs, and was more interested in granting amnesty, visas and green cards than jobs for *"middle class folks"* and American college graduates.

Also, the Supreme Court decided it was unconstitutional to ban corporations and unions from pumping money into political ads. [844] The Center for Public Integrity (CPI) worried this decision could be exploited by foreign nations such as China, Saudi Arabia, Singapore, Venezuela and more that had bought US companies. [844] Another risk is corporate "contributions" from US companies with foreign investors. CPI noted that in such cases it would be difficult to determine if foreign money was being used to influence our elections. [844]

One of the greatest threats to the integrity of our elections is internet voting: *"experts say no one will be certain those votes haven't been tampered with"* wrote Ed Barnes in a 2012 *FoxNews* story "Internet Voting Arrives...But is it Secret and Safe." To illustrate the vulnerability he reported that Washington DC opened a new electronic voting system for the public to test. In just hours, University of Michigan hackers testing security took over the system. Another big surprise-they were not alone. *A computer in China and a computer in Iran* were hacking the system. John Bonifax, legal director of Voter Action said, *"It showed that it wasn't just a domestic problem of vote security but a matter of national security."* [899]

How did foreign nations know the system was being tested? The security on Internet voting can be like those silly cartoons where there is a door with no walls. What good is a locked door for security when hackers can just go around the door? We need to find a more secure and private way to tabulate votes.

Chapter 13

Freedom of Religion

Religion defines a culture.

Revisionist history has been used to hijack our democracy. They misconstrue our forefathers meaning for freedom of religion and separation of church and state.

To understand what our forefathers meant by "freedom of religion" you have to look at their history. The drafters of the US Constitution were English. They did not want the new government to exercise any power over the church as their ancestors had experienced in England. For example, William Tyndale was killed for translating the Bible from Greek to English. The Church of England wanted control, and did not want the people to read the Bible. Christians wanted to read the Bible for themselves.

The American Revolution was not about just money. Many of our founders were people of property who put their financial security as well as their lives on the line to fight for freedom.

As Patrick Henry said, "I know not what course others may take, but as for me, give me liberty or give me death." He also explained "freedom of religion", ":...*all men are equally entitled to the free exercise of religion, according to the dictates of conscience; and that it is the mutual duty of all to practice Christian forbearance, love, and charity towards each other.*"

US Christian Cultural Foundation

Religion defines cultures around the world. Major life events are centered around religion. Our culture was defined by the Christian religion. From the founding of our nation, we marked major life events in our churches. In Christian churches we were baptized, married the person we loved, and said farewell to loved ones who completed their journey in this world. From the opening prelude, to the melodious hymn, to the solemn amen, it defined the song of our life on earth.

"Jesus in China," a 2008 PBS special by Frontline/World, reported that a prominent Chinese economist, Zhao Xiao, traveled to the United States to discover the secret of our success. He found the answer was Jesus. Following Christian principles were the key to a flourishing business environment. Zhao converted to Christianity and wrote an article, "God is my Chairman of the Board." He encouraged the Communist Party to also find Christianity. [710] Zhao's discovery reaffirmed what George Washington said in his farewell address.

When George Washington took the oath of office as the first President of the United States he did not put his hand on the Constitution. He did not put his hand on a stack of religious books. He placed his hand on only one book–the Holy Bible. In Washington's Farewell Address he explained why: *"Where is the security for property, for reputation, for life, if the sense of religious obligation desert the oaths, which are the instruments of investigation in courts of Justice? ...reason and experience both forbid us to expect, that national morality can prevail in exclusion of religious principle."* He spoke of one religion: *"With slight shades of difference, you have the same religion, manners, habits, and political principles."* [660] The religion he spoke of as essential to preservation of our country was Christianity. His Bible is on display at Mount Vernon. *Not one of our outspoken forefathers objected to his taking the oath on the Bible.*

The Battle Cry of the American Revolution was, "No king, but King Jesus," and the source was Reverend Jonas Clarke. (Also see I Timothy 6: 14-15.) Their call to liberty came from the Bible, Galatians 5:1. The eagle as national symbol was also from the Bible, Isaiah 40:31. The first prayer in Congress on September 7, 1774, by Jacob Duche concluded with, *"all this we ask in the Name and through the merits of Jesus Christ, Thy Son and our Savior."* [829] Look up the song "America"–Who is the "Author of Liberty"?

Our forefathers who drafted and adopted the Constitution knew better than anyone the meaning of the Constitution.

John Adams said, *"Our Constitution was made only for a moral and religious people. It is wholly inadequate to the government of any other."*

James Madison who wrote our Constitution in 1787, and is often called the "Father of the Constitution" explained: *"We have staked the whole future of the American civilization, not upon the power of government, far from it. We have staked the future of all of our political institutions upon the capacity of mankind to <u>self-government upon the capacity of each and all of us to govern ourselves, to control ourselves, to sustain ourselves according to the Ten Commandments of God</u>."*

The founding fathers had witnesses in our nation's courts swear to tell the truth by placing their hand on the Bible because it is the foundation of our government and laws.

Franklin D. Roosevelt, in his D-Day Prayer also referenced "our religion" not religions. *"Almighty God: Our sons, pride of our nation, this day have set upon a mighty endeavor, a struggle to preserve our Republic, <u>our religion</u>, and our civilization, and to set free a suffering humanity."* [667] The graves marked with crosses in Normandy provide a solid silent witness that our heritage is Christian.

Restore Our Cultural Roots

Revisionist history spawned in our universities is misleading our youth. *In a nation founded by Christians so they could be free from religious persecution, we now see persecution of Christians.* We are losing the freedom of religion for which our forefathers fought.

Universities such as Harvard, Yale, Duke, and Princeton were founded as Christian colleges. Yet, it appears that Christian Protestants are discriminated against and underrepresented in our universities.

Most non-Christian religions are incompatible with our cultural values such as equality, freedom of religion, liberty of the people, and the Christian work ethic.

Recall what Soros wrote: *"Societies derive their cohesion from shared values. The values are rooted in culture, religion, history, and tradition."* [932] His takeover of our nation with his open society can only be done if we abandon our Christian culture. Also, recall Stalin's strategy: *"America is like a healthy body and its resistance is threefold: its patriotism, its morality, and its spiritual life. If we can undermine these three areas, America will collapse from within."*

Our forefathers' concept of freedom of religion was based on following the example of Christ who invited people, of their free will, to follow him. You decide if you believe. You decide if you want to go to church. You chose which church to attend. You decide if you pray and when you pray. You, not the government, decide how much money to give to the church.

The Christian foundation for freedom of religion is also explained in the Bible, for example Romans Chapter 14. Most of our founding fathers were devout Christians. Some were not. It was all a matter of free choice.

Until recent times, the Christian religion was a part of our public schools. Often the church and school were in the same building. Christians emphasized education because they wanted their children to be able to read the Bible. Students in public schools read the Bible, sang Christian songs, and produced Christmas programs with nativity scenes and more. For example, watch the school Christmas program scene in the 1947 Cary Grant movie, "Penny Serenade."

We are told that our nation is progressing. Is that true? Are our children happier? Will they have a better future? By most objective observations our nation is declining and our freedoms grow dim. What some call "progressive" is the destruction of our culture and our families. We have lost sight of the wisdom of our forefathers. They drew their strength and guidance from the Bible. They were not perfect, but they built a nation that achieved freedom and the pursuit of happiness that is rare to find in this world. What is the fruit of a Christian culture: "*The fruit of the Spirit is love, joy, peace, patience, kindness, goodness, faithfulness, gentleness, and self-control.*" Galatians 5:22, 34.

We need to reclaim our cultural roots.

Chapter 14

True Immigration Reform

"I hereby declare, on oath, that I absolutely and <u>entirely renounce and abjure all allegiance and fidelity to any foreign prince, potentate, state, or sovereignty</u> of who or which I have heretofore been a subject or citizen; that I will support and defend the Constitution and laws of the United States of America against all enemies, foreign and domestic; that <u>I will bear true faith and allegiance to the same</u>..." [713]-United States Oath of Citizenship

Our nation has benefited greatly from immigrants who admire our nation's history and culture and want to become Americans and meld with our society. When immigrants share their stories of oppression, it reminds us of the huge debt we owe to our forefathers.

A controlled immigration policy that carefully screens applicants and allows about 200,000 immigrants per year is beneficial to our country, and welcomed by most Americans.

However, our nation has been flooded by immigrants who show no allegiance to our country. *Some immigrants are divisive and band together to benefit their ethnic group and country of origin to the detriment of our country and Americans not in their ethnic group.* They attack our culture, religion, history and traditions, and seize control of our government through ethnic lobbies that seek fraudulent visa programs and amnesty opposed by US citizens.

True Intentions of Our Forefathers

The intention of our Founding Fathers was to build a Christian nation *where they and their descendents* could live in freedom and prosperity. It was not their vision to build an open borders multicultural and multifaith nation of immigrants who denigrated their culture and faith, and took the inheritance they built for their progeny. The US Constitution clearly states:

- "*We the People of the United States, in Order to form a more perfect Union establish Justice, insure domestic Tranquility, provide for the common defense, promote the general Welfare, and secure the Blessings of Liberty to ourselves and our Posterity, do ordain and establish this Constitution for the United States of America.*"

A GREAT GENERATION CARRIED THE TORCH OF FREEDOM

Americans who grew up during the Great Depression and rose up out of the ashes of Pearl Harbor to fight and win World War II are true heroes. After the war it was their ingenuity and resolve that made our country the most advanced and powerful nation in the world. Like our founding fathers, they too were *determined to provide a better life for their children than they had.*

In a stunning act of Christian forgiveness and generosity they helped rebuild the very nations that tried to destroy them.

Moreover, they gave aid to people around the world. They brought foreign students here to study so that they could return to their countries and build thriving communities. Never did they suspect that some foreign students would come to our nation as guests with the intention of violating our immigration laws and forming ethnic lobbies that robbed their children and grandchildren of their inheritance.

Zero Population Growth Goal

While our nation has been generous in welcoming new immigrants, our immigration has grown out of control. Overpopulation is one of the biggest threats the world is facing. It causes scarcity, pollution, and poverty.

In the 1950's, countries around the world were warned of dire consequences if they failed to control population growth. Determined to control population growth, Americans opposed any increases in the number of immigrants per year. [275] Then in the 1960's *Americans set the goal of zero population growth*, and decreased the size of their families with the aim of providing a better future for their children.

Yet, our government increased immigration. As a result, already in some regions of our country the consumption rate of fresh water is 10 times faster than it can be replenished. [702] Mass immigration to the US will not solve overpopulation problems in foreign countries. What it will do is overpopulate the US, and plunge the US into poverty.

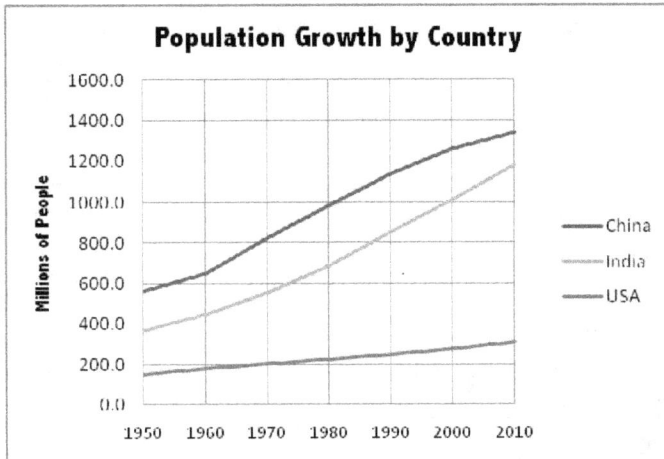

Population Growth by Country

India and China continued massive population increases despite all the warnings. [563] Most US population growth is from immigration.

Congress Acted Against the Will of US Citizens

Why did our immigration gush out of control like a broken fire hydrant? Lobbies for foreign governments and groups making money from immigration tipped our political scales. Against the will of US citizens, that they were under oath to represent, Congress set off a population explosion in the United States with these three pieces of legislation:

- *Immigration Act of 1965*
- *Amnesty in 1986*
- *Non-immigrant H-1B visa program in 1990 that was exploited for massive immigration from India, China, and Muslim countries.*

Dr. Norm Matloff, a critic of the H-1B visas, wrote that *US immigration policy is "set by a small group of Washington insiders who are unknown to the general public but who ... often profit from their inside status, through jobs, contracts and so on."* He noted: *"What we have, then, is a classic example of people writing laws and then taking lucrative jobs in the private sector which benefit from those laws."* [24]

Our politicians even passed an investor visa program that *gave green cards to wealthy foreigners who invested $1 million in a US company.* Former INS officials set up companies that collected millions of dollars in fees. Some were *sued for defrauding the US government by getting green cards for foreigners who only paid a fraction of the amount required.* [276] Did foreign investors in outsourcing companies, and foreign oil money buy green cards?

Our government is admitting more immigrants per year than all the European countries combined! Over a million "legal" foreign immigrants a year now flood into the United States. [274]

Ironically, Americans who limited their family size to create a better future for their children, instead put their children's future at risk because many of the new immigrants formed ethnic networks for political and business power.

Immigration Act of 1965-Congress Lied

US citizens opposed the Immigration Act of 1965. This law abandoned the over 180 year old immigration policy of our forefathers who favored immigration from countries that shared their cultural values. Congress passed it anyway.

Senator Strom Thurmond voted against the bill because of overpopulation concerns. And, Myra C. Hacker, VP of a New Jersey Coalition, testified at a Senate subcommittee:

■ *"In light of our 5% unemployment rate, our <u>worries over the so called population explosion</u>, and our menacingly mounting welfare costs...At the very least, <u>the hidden mathematics of the bill should be made clear to the public</u> so that they may tell their Congressmen how they feel about providing jobs, schools, homes,...for an indeterminately enormous number of aliens from underprivileged lands. ...Whatever may be our benevolent intent toward many people (the bill) <u>fails to give due consideration to the economic needs, the cultural traditions, and the public sentiment of the citizens of the United States.</u>"* [994]

However, Senator Edward Kennedy promised:

■ *"First, our cities <u>**will not be flooded with a million immigrants annually**</u>. Under the proposed bill, the present level of immigration remains substantially the same...Secondly, <u>the ethnic mix of this country will not be upset...It will not cause American workers to lose their jobs.</u>"* [994] *Both were not true.*

Secretary of State Dean Rusk reassured:

■ *"The present estimate...is that there might be say, 8,000 immigrants from India in the next five years..."* [994]

Senator Hiram Fong promised limited Asian immigration:

■ *"Our people from that part of the world will never reach 1 percent of the population. <u>Our cultural pattern will never be changed as far as America is concerned.</u>"* [994]

Senator Claiborne Pell guaranteed:

- *"Contrary to the opinions of some of the misinformed, this legislation does not open the flood gates."* [994]

Sponsors claimed this law was for "equality" to end discrimination. Yet, it granted non-white immigrants "minority" privileges. So a white child, whose father, grandfather ... helped build our nation, was discriminated against, while children whose ancestors did nothing to build our nation received favored privileges. This law caused a "minority" explosion that unfairly burdened US taxpayers, and cheated deserving US minorities, descendents of slaves and native tribes, out of educational, job, and business startup opportunities.

The law opened the door to college educated foreigners who were supposed to have *"exceptional ability."*

- *India's non-resident Indians credit the 1965 immigration law, and the "American economy revved up by the Vietnam War" for <u>opening the door to jobs at US military contractors, NASA and US universities.</u>* [187] *So, our government sent young Americans off to the Vietnam War, while at the same time it gave strategic high paying technology jobs to young foreigners their age.*

<u>*Congress promised the number of immigrants admitted per year would not increase.*</u> However, Congress added *"family chain migration"* to the 1965 law. *This let each new immigrant sponsor: their parents, spouse, children, and siblings.* In turn their spouse could then sponsor his/her parents and siblings. Next, each of the spouse's siblings could sponsor their spouse and children. The 1965 law did not limit the number of children and siblings, or the number of links.

The following Family Chain Migration diagram for simplicity computes 3 children and 4 siblings per immigrant family. Of course family sizes vary.

Family Chain Migration = Out-of-Control Immigration
Example of First 3 Links

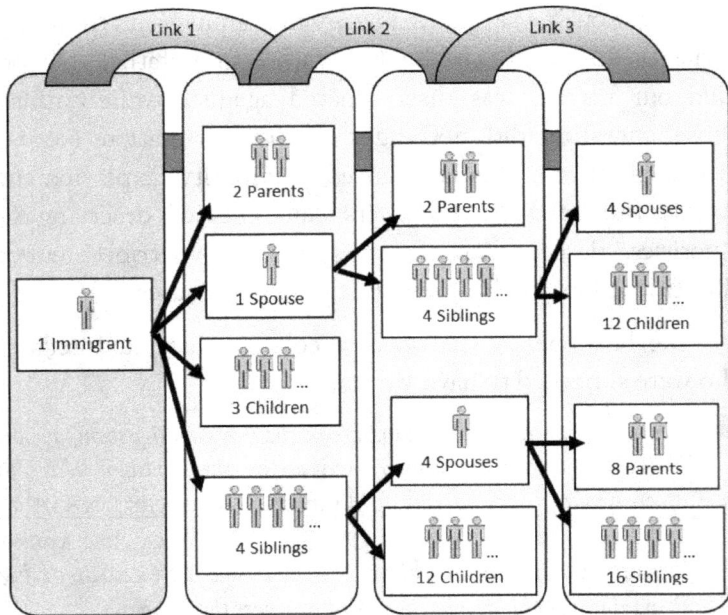

In the above example, one immigration slot is filled. Family Chain migration triggered by the new immigrant for the first 3 Links totals: 10 (Link 1) + 22 (Link 2) + 40 (Link 3) = 72 additional "legal" immigrants. The Chain goes on and on to Link 4, Link 5... Family Chain Migration lets one immigrant channel in an uncontrolled number of more immigrants. *If this is not stopped our children will become a minority in their own country.*

If chain migration continues it will cause *an estimated 100 million increase* in our population by 2060. [1041]

1986 Amnesty = Big Mistake

The 1965 immigration law with chain migration spawned a flood of "legal" immigrants from impoverished countries. While some embraced our culture and fit right in, others formed divisive ethnic networks.

Additionally, scores harbored illegals, often relatives such as an uncle or cousin, from their country of origin. So, by 1986 *about 128,000 illegals per year were entering our country. As their numbers grew* Congress was pressured by illegal aliens and their relatives to grant an amnesty.

Americans said no amnesty. It rewards disrespecting our borders and breaking our laws.

Congress claimed amnesty would end the illegal immigration problem, and passed the Immigration Reform and Control Act of 1986. There was no reform.

The 1986 law granted amnesty to approximately 3 million illegal aliens. But that is not all; our government secretly *allowed people granted amnesty to apply for "family chain migration," and as a result "legal" immigration soared to over a million a year!*

Our government also hid from Americans, that about 10% of the illegal aliens granted amnesty in 1986 were visa violators overstaying student, travel, and worker visas. These illegals were primarily from China, India, and Muslim nations.

As Americans warned, *the 1986 amnesty made illegal immigration worse*. Many people granted amnesty, showed no allegiance to our nation and flagrantly broke our immigration laws again by channeling in and harboring illegals from their country of origin.

By 2003 about 700,000 illegal aliens were invading our country each year over a 400% increase of the rate before the 1986 amnesty. [143]

H-1B Act 1990 – Opposed by Americans

Executives sold the 1990 H-1B program to Congress as a *non-immigrant visa* (NIV) to *temporarily* fill high tech US worker shortages. The shortages never existed.

US citizens were kept in the dark. When Americans learned about this legislation they strongly opposed it.

The main H-1B benefactor was India:

- *People from India living the US "saw it (H-1B) as a means of increasing immigration from their homeland, while providing them with engineers who shared language, culture and customs with them, not just academic training, and most importantly, would work for less money." [121] (indolink.com report)*

- *H-1B "temporary" visa workers from India often brought a spouse and their parents. [289]*

The demographic impact of the H-1B is predominantly Hindus and Muslims from India, Muslims from Pakistan, and Buddhists from China took American jobs from Christians and took minority job opportunities that should have gone to black Americans. From 1990-2001, the number of Hindus living in the United States increased 237%, Muslims increased 109% and Buddhists increased 170%. [714]

Following the dotcom crash in 2000, we had high unemployment, yet immigration from India accelerated. In 2007, a "Non-Resident Indian and Person of Indian Origin," entry on Wikipedia claimed: *"From 2000 onwards the growth rate and the per cent rate of Indians amongst all the immigrants has increased by over 100 times."* H-1Bs took jobs from American programmers, engineers, accountants, doctors.... the American Association of Physicians of Indian Origin swelled to a membership of 35,000. [618] How many got a US education subsidized by our tax dollars? Many qualified Americans cannot afford the cost of medical school.

Formula for Disaster-Multiplier Effect

The 1965 immigration law with chain migration, multiplied by the 1986 amnesty, and compounded by the 1990 "non-immigrant" H-1B program created an uncontrolled immigration explosion. Prior to this, *from 1925 - 1965 the United States averaged admitting 178,000 immigrants per year.* [143] By 2003, our government was admitting almost 1.1 million "legal" immigrants per year. [143]

From 1990-2000, the number of foreign-born people living in the USA surged from 13 million to 32 million. Only about 9 million were "legal" immigrants. [397] [272] They competed with citizens for jobs, overcrowded our schools, increased healthcare costs, and drove up energy costs. In 2001, after the dotcom crash, our government knew we had high unemployment, yet it issued 1.2 million *non-immigrant visas*, and granted 1.1 million green cards. [28] [274] While war diverted our attention, immigration surged to about 4 million per year!

Our Government Promised No Increase-- But Immigration Increased 20 Fold!

2001	Family Chain & 1986 Amnesty	Green Cards	Non-Immigrant Visas	Illegals

| 1965 | 200,000 yr. Promised No Increase |

| 0 | 1,000,000 | 2,000,000 | 3,000,000 | 4,000,000 |

Number of "legal" and illegal Immigrants per year

Immigration Drives Up Health Care Costs

Our government's failure to control immigration played a big role in our current healthcare crisis. Healthcare is not free. It is very expensive. *Ironically, a key reason companies offshore our jobs is to evade rising healthcare costs caused by immigration.*

There are two parts to this problem. First, we have the low skilled poor immigrants who have no insurance. The number of uninsured immigrants jumped from 2.2 million in 1997, to 11.2 million in 2002. [275] Second, we have foreign visa workers who took jobs and insurance away from millions of college educated Americans. As a result many families of highly skilled well educated Americans have no insurance.

Foreigners Sue for US Citizenship!

The number of applications for US citizenship became unmanageable. Foreigners had the audacity to sue the US Citizenship and Immigration Services (USCIS) for delays in approving their applications. The number of lawsuits grew rapidly from 270 lawsuits in 2005, to 4,400 in 2007.

The USCIS is required to run background checks and to make sure applicants are not on terrorism or criminal watch lists. [676] [672] In 2007, USCIS received 1.4 million naturalization applications for US citizenship! [672] Because of its work overload, *the USCIS changed its policy to automatically grant green cards if the applicant has been waiting for more than six months. If a criminal or terrorist got a green card, the Department of Homeland Security could revoke the green card and begin deportation proceedings.* [672] This is a dangerous policy change.

Processing all these citizenship applications cost over $32 million per year. [672] Why should US citizens be taxed to pay for harmful increases in immigration they do not want?

Anchor Babies = Misuse of 14ᵗʰ Amendment

It's actually worse than a 20 fold increase in immigration because that number does not count *"anchor babies."* Babies born to non-citizens in the US are called *"anchor babies"* since foreigners use these babies to attempt to gain US citizenship. *Estimates run as high as 1 in 10 births are to non-citizens.* [846] In 2009, illegals gave birth to about 300,000 babies in the US; plus, you may be surprised to learn, foreign women on student visas, H-1B visas, travel visas and other temporary visas gave birth to 200,000. That's ½ million anchor babies in one year!

The 14ᵗʰ Amendment states: *"All persons born or naturalized in the United States, and <u>subject to the jurisdiction thereof</u>, are citizens of the United States and of the state wherein they reside."* The intention was to grant citizenship to freed slaves who had no other country. Senator Jacob Merritt Howard of Michigan added *"subject to the jurisdiction"* to make it clear that, *<u>"this will not, of course, include persons born in the United States who are foreigners, aliens, who belong to the families of ambassadors or foreign ministers ..."</u>* [845] <u>Interpreting this Amendment to give babies different citizenship than their parents is absurd. The drafters certainly did not intend that babies be taken from their parents, nor did they intend that having a baby in our country would mean foreigners could stay.</u> Moreover, US laws recognize that babies born abroad inherit their US parents' citizenship. [605]

A 2011, article, "Dvorak: Immigration Think Tank Sees Birthright Citizenship as Threat to U.S. Security," warned that Anwar al Awlaki who directed *"terrorist attacks against America,"* and Yaser Esam Hamdi an *"enemy combatant captured in Afghanistan"* were anchor babies. [940]

Over a seven year people while we have been at war Turkish women on tourist visas have given birth to 12,000 babies in our country. [846]

"Birthing Centers for Chinese Women Looking to Have American Babies Uncovered in California," a 2011 *Fox News* report said that Chinese women were coming to the US "*to give birth to US citizens.*" These may include babies of communist party leaders. Lawmakers were outraged at the "*abuse of the Constitution's 14th Amendment,*" and wanted to change our laws. [903] They need to enforce the law as it was originally intended.

Millions of babies were born to H-1Bs since this fraudulent "temporary" visa legislation was passed in 1990. Some of their anchor babies are 23 years old now–did they get minority scholarships and jobs? An empathetic 2004 PBS story on an H-1B from India who lost his job said he and his wife stayed until their baby was born. [902] Who paid the hospital? They returned to India. But, a 2009 update said they were back in the US even though we had high unemployment. *Where were PBS empathetic stories for young Americans graduating from college who cannot afford to get married and have a baby because H-1Bs take entry level US jobs?*

Huma Abedin is an anchor baby whose Indian Islamic father and Pakistani Islamic mother were here as college professors when she was born. When Abedin was 2 they moved to Saudi Arabia. Abedin returned to the US to attend college. In 1996, Abedin became an intern to first lady Hillary Clinton. [938] (Clinton's 1996 SUV "stimulus" was a windfall for Saudis.) Of all the young Americans, how was a Muslim anchor baby reared in Saudi Arabia by non-American parents picked for such a desirable and sensitive assignment? This was a stepping stone. "*Weiner's Mother-in-Law a member of Muslim Brotherhood: Tasked with Advancing Movement that Aims to Establish Saudi-style Regime in U.S*" a 2011 WND report said that Abedin's chief of staff job for Secretary of State Hillary Clinton gave her access to state secrets, and the "inner workings of Congress." [938]

True Immigration Reform

New immigrants should be treated fairly and with respect. And, we need to welcome them as part of our community. However, our government needs better screening methods that assure citizenship is only granted to individuals who value our cultural heritage and will be loyal to the United States.

Out of control immigration is a formula for disaster. During times of high unemployment, war, pandemics, or other major crisis, immigration needs to be stopped or greatly reduced.

Congress promised Americans in 1965 that the number of immigrants admitted per year would not increase. Then they flooded our nation with millions annually granting citizenship, green cards, and visas. It is time to repeal family chain migration. Congress needs to honor their promise, and cap the number of immigrants admitted per year to 200,000.

Anchor baby abuse needs to stop. Children belong with their parents and naturally have the same citizenship as their parents. Our government has no right to tax US citizens, who want to have their own children, instead to pay for the birth and support of foreigners' children. Americans cannot afford to pay for medical care, twelve years of public education, and even college expenses for millions of children who should not legally even be in our country.

Congress promised that our culture would not be changed by immigration. Yet, they allowed textbooks to be altered with anti-American anti-Christian text to appease immigrants from other cultures. In schools and universities our forefathers are denigrated, and some students object to the US flag. School Christmas songs and plays, a key part of our culture since the founding of our nation, are banned as is prayer to not offend immigrants of other religions.

Congress promised the ethnic mix of our nation would be unchanged. Not only has the ethnic mix dramatically changed, ethnic lobbies benefit new immigrants and their countries of origin at the expense of the descendents of pre 1965 US citizens.

In 1907, Theodore Roosevelt emphasized the benefits of US citizenship were predicated on *"becoming in very fact an American, and nothing but an American."* [457] Yet consider, in January 2010, Professor Jagdish Bhagwati delivered a speech, "The Role of the Diaspora" in New Delhi, India. He wanted India's diaspora with dual US citizenship to pay "a Bhagwati tax" to India *"their mother country."* He wanted India's diaspora to be allowed to vote in India's elections. [887]

It is unjust for our government to enslave Americans to pay for minority benefits and entitlements for new immigrants. New immigrants need to follow the historic American work ethic and support themselves.

If you look around the world, the nations promoting the diversity agenda for the US do not apply the same standard to their own nation. How many immigrants do they accept per year? Can Americans immigrate: hold government jobs, run for president, have access to government databases and scientific research, get minority privileges? Does their nation allow freedom of religion and welcome Christian immigrants?

Americans have the right, as do people in other nations, to decide how much immigration we want and on the qualifications required to become a citizen. It would be a sad thing to lose the culture of the US which has generated prosperity and elevated the people, and sent aid to other countries around the world.

Chapter 15

Another Amnesty will Collapse

US

Amnesty rewards the wrong people.

Why do we have an illegal alien problem? Our government failed to protect our borders. We are paying billions of dollars on defense, and yet there are between 12–21 million illegal aliens in our country. [664] Having a hundred people in our country illegally would be bad, but up to 21 million shows an utter disregard for US citizens they are sworn to protect.

A retired INS investigator and intelligence specialist, Michael W. Cutler, criticized the Obama Administration: "*It is clear that the marching orders coming from the administration have nothing to do with securing our nation's borders or enforcing the immigration laws.*" And he notes that it is absurd to think the war on terrorism can succeed when terrorists can easily cross our borders and, "*embed themselves in our nation with virtually no fear of being identified, arrested or removed from our country.*" [874]

Our government has an obligation to enforce immigration laws. Granting amnesty is not immigration reform.

People on entitlements need to think about what they are doing if they press for another amnesty. If our nation collapses, all their benefits will be lost.

Another Amnesty Will Collapse Our Country

Our economy cannot support another amnesty. The 1986 amnesty increased illegal immigration almost fourfold. If another amnesty causes a fourfold increase, illegal immigration will jump from about 700,000 per year rate to 2,800,000! Moreover, if our government grants amnesty and allows them to apply for family chain migration, like it did in 1986, then legal immigration can be expected to explode to 5 times the current rate to over 5 million per year!

No country in the world could survive 2.8 million illegals per year crossing borders to get free medical, educational, and other services plus, 5 million legal immigrants who will strain our scarce resources and infrastructure and compete with Americans for jobs.

"ICE Agents Vote 'No Confidence' in Leaders"

In July 2001, one INS manager, was quoted as saying, *"Our job is to explain to people why they are here illegally, help them change that, and help them to get benefits."* [143] That is not the role of the INS.

In August 2010, The Washington Times article, "ICE Agents Vote 'No Confidence' in Leaders, Say Amnesty Coming," reported that the 10% increase in deportation, is a farce because illegal aliens in jail *"seek out ICE agents for deportation to avoid prosecution, conviction and prison terms...criminal aliens "openly brag" that they are taking advantage of a broken immigration system and will be back in the United States within days to commit crimes—while US citizens arrested for the same offenses serve prison sentences."* [874] Deportation = get out of jail free; and then, start violating our immigration laws all over again.

Cover-up of Illegal Alien Crime Statistics

Our news media is failing to report that illegal aliens in some areas of our country account for "12% of felonies, 25% of burglaries and 34% of thefts. *Over one fourth of the criminals in our federal prisons were illegal aliens. In Los Angeles County alone incarcerated illegal aliens cost $150 million a year.*" [275] Think of what the cost must be nationally.

Leaders in our government have stood in the way of INS reform. In his 2003, book "Who's Looking Out for You?" Bill O'Reilly exposed leaders in our capital *"know that the government's failure to control illegal immigration has directly led to the murders of Americans and to billions of dollars in related expenses. Twelve percent of all incarcerated felons in California are illegal aliens. The damage inflicted on America by uncontrolled immigration is incalculateable."* [872]

Amnesty Rewards the Wrong People

Immigrants who followed all the rules and respected our nation's borders to obtain citizenship demonstrated a respect for our nation and our laws. Such law abiding immigrants are a welcome and valuable addition to our country.

However, if someone is in our country illegally, their actions show disrespect for our nation and a propensity to break laws. To work here they have to break more laws to obtain fake social security numbers, driver's licenses, and other fraudulent documents. If they paid to be smuggled across our border, then they are more likely to attempt to smuggle and sell drugs. Or, if they committed visa fraud, they are more likely to commit white collar crimes such as stock market fraud, or intellectual property theft. One crime leads to the next, including illegally influencing US elections to get amnesty and minority benefits.

DREAM Act = Economic Nightmare

The "DREAM Act" for illegal aliens will deny young Americans their American dream. American college graduates face a dismal job market. Some statistics report that up to 55% have to move back in with their parents because they cannot find jobs. If their parents lost their jobs to foreign workers, and in turn defaulted on their mortgage, moving home may not even be an option.

Why is the "DREAM Act" an economic nightmare? The key is the college loan debt crisis. In 2010 student loan debt soared to $800 billion exceeding US credit card debt. In 2011 *student loan debt surpassed a trillion dollars!* [1067] Throw in the "DREAM Act" allowing foreigners to take jobs from young Americans, and *it will set off an avalanche of student loan defaults. Already, in the first two months of 2013 student loan defaults hit $3 billion. The rate of defaults was rapidly accelerating with a 36% jump over 2012.*

A *New York Times* blog in 2010, "'Eerie Echo' of Mortgage Crises in Student Loan Debt," tells how our kids will be denied the American dream of buying a home because they are saddled with college loans that will take them decades to repay. [914]

In baseball, its one, two, three strikes and you are out.

The dotcom crash was strike one against our nation. It was a manipulation of both our stock market by foreign "investors," and our job market by foreign graduates wanting American jobs.

The housing crisis was strike two. It was an *'eerie echo'* of the dotcom crash. When Americans lost their jobs, they could not make house payments so they lost their homes to foreclosures.

If not reversed, Obama's 2012 DREAM Act Executive Order will be strike three. [1068] Our economy cannot withstand another big hit. It will collapse.

ILLEGAL ASIANS IN OUR PUBLIC SCHOOLS

In 2010, high school age Asian students, in the US illegally, protested and called themselves: "DREAM Act Immigration Activists." According to an article in *asianweek.com*, *"millions of hard-working students in the United States... do not qualify for state or federal grants, and are unable to afford college."* They point out the misconception that undocumented students in our public schools are all Latinos. The article says *"they are united as one to fight for their rights."* They formed Asian Students Promoting Immigrant Rights through Education (ASPIRE).

They acknowledged that Rep. Lamar Smith said the DREAM Act was a *"nightmare for the American people."* [925]

DRIVING FORCE "GLUT" OF COLLEGE GRADS IN CHINA & INDIA

The driving force for outsourcing was an excess of college educated workers in India and China, not a shortage in the US, according to a 2004 government report that was withheld from Americans. It got worse. A "China's College Graduate Glut," report in the *China Economic Review* said *4.95 million were graduating in 2007 which was 5 times the number China graduated in 2000*! It warned: *"There are simply too many of them to absorb even for a growing economy like China."* [917] The glut was even bigger in India. For example, the Indian outsourcing firm Infosys had 1.5 million applicants apply for 25,000 jobs in 2007. That is *60 people for every job!* [916]

This glut of college graduates in Asia is the big hidden driving force behind the "DREAM Act." They flood into US graduate schools on student visas, and then try to get an H-1B or other work visa. If they do not get a work visa, or if their work visa expires, most stay illegally. [143] So *young Americans with undergraduate degrees and huge college debt are forced to compete for American jobs against older foreign graduate students that we subsidized*. Our kids don't stand a fair chance.

ACT NOW TO STOP CONGRESS

The "DREAM Act" will destroy US colleges because it will create a US glut of graduates making college degrees worthless; and, it will deny jobs to Americans who fund our colleges through taxes, paying college tuition, and making donations.

The media calls adult illegals up to 35 years old *"innocent children."* These "children" committed felonies if they engaged in identity theft stealing American's social security numbers or falsifying documents to get drivers' license and vote in our elections. How are they victims? They cost taxpayers about $120,000 per student for twelve years of school. Many also got free lunches and medical care. Instead of thanking us and offering to repay us, they demand we pay for their college. The real victims are Americans.

Senator Dick Durbin submitted the DREAM Act in 2001, and it was defeated in 2007. [875] In 2010 Durbin had help from *Harry Reid who was up for reelection and vowed to get a lame duck session "DREAM Act" vote.* Reid won despite polls showing Sharron Angle in the lead. Some voters complained Reid's name was pre-checked on electronic ballots. [919] Reid brought the "DREAM Act" to a vote. It was defeated again.

· In June 2011, Durbin led a "DREAM Act" hearing in the *"the largest hearing room in the Senate."* Hundreds of illegal aliens were invited *"to openly participate in the proceedings."* Janet Napolitano had a front row seat. Durbin said, *"Over the years, I have met hundreds of these dreamers, and hundreds of them are here today."* He called them by name as *he* told their personal stories. [931] How many young Americans has Durbin met with? Can he tell their personal stories of struggles to repay college debt and to find a job?

To his credit, Durbin has worked with Senator Grassley to end H-1B fraud. But, does he not realize H-1B fraud sprang from foreign students who wanted to take US jobs?

Visa Violators Number in the Millions

The 1986 amnesty *"immigration reform"* for 3 million illegals failed. It did not end illegal immigration. By 2008, we had an estimated 20 million illegals! [664] Visa violators increased from 10% in 1986 to about *40% of illegals in our country today.*

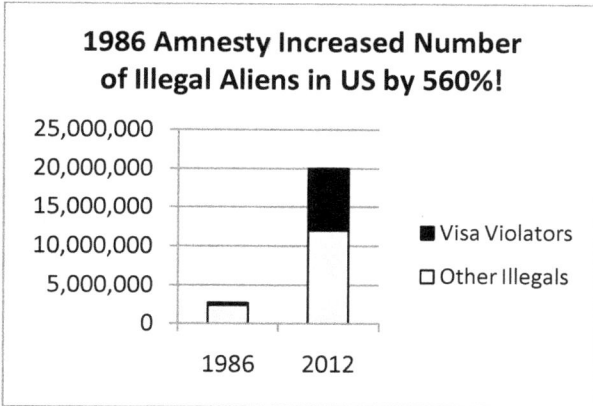

1986 Amnesty Increased Number of Illegal Aliens in US by 560%!

A bar chart showing two stacked bars for 1986 and 2012. The y-axis ranges from 0 to 25,000,000 in increments of 5,000,000. The 1986 bar is small. The 2012 bar reaches about 20,000,000, with a lower "Other Illegals" (white) portion of about 11,000,000 and an upper "Visa Violators" (black) portion above it.

Legend: ■ Visa Violators   □ Other Illegals

1986   2012

Illegal Alien Tax—Should be Illegal

Generations ago our forefather fought against "taxation without representation." How can "representatives" legally spend our tax money set aside for Americans' retirement, education, welfare, medical care and more on illegal aliens? [60]

A Heritage Foundation study in 2007 found that illegal aliens' households headed by low-skill workers cost a net tax loss of $22,449 each per year. It warned; *"Over the next ten years the total cost of low-skill households to the taxpayer (immediate benefits minus taxes paid) is likely to be at least $3.9 trillion."* [657]

The *Federation for American Immigration Reform* (FAIR) predicted in 2010 that an amnesty would overburden Social Security and public assistance costs. *The biggest expense was $52 billion to educate the children of illegals.* [850] Of course such estimates vary. Some do not include the cost to educate anchor babies.

Globally Our Children are Left Behind!

In 1982, the US Supreme Court decided (Plyler v. Doe) to force US taxpayers to finance the education of the children of illegal aliens. The decision *barely passed with a narrow 5 to 4 margin.* [459] The decision was based on the "pivotal role" public education plays in *"sustaining our political and cultural heritage."* [459] Illegal aliens do not sustain our political and cultural heritage, they undermine it.

Our government should be looking out for the innocent children of Americans who lost their jobs to foreign workers. Parents' job losses obviously will impact their children's performance in school. It's a dual blow of stress and a disincentive. Our global standing is negatively impacted: *"the quality of education in math and science in elementary and high school has plummeted, leading to a drop in the number of students majoring in technical fields in college and graduate school."* [553] We are paying more for education– *the cost per pupil has more than quadrupled since the 1980's.* [275] Yet, the US Department of Education, the National Center for Education Statistics, and the Program for International Student Assessment, reported *US students scores ranked below 20 countries in math and 13 countries in science.* [615]

The "No Child Left Behind" penalizes teachers if white students are the top performers in their class. It is cruel and unjust for young white students, many whose parents lost jobs because of visa fraud, to see post 1965 immigrants get minority scholarships and awards because they are not white. Schools can "narrow the gap" by raising the low performers and/or, by lowering the top performers. *Attempts to narrow the gap for students not proficient in English was costing us $10,000 more per student annually just to bring them up to average level.* [275] But, *the biggest cost is that globally our children and our nation are left behind when our educational system is crippled by out of control immigration.*

Nation of Immigrants Propaganda

Illegal aliens call the US a "Nation of Immigrants" to justify breaking our immigration laws. This excuse is unfounded given:

- *First, if mankind's origins track to Africa, then all nations, other than Africa, are nations of immigrants.*

- *Second, early settlers arrived at a harsh wilderness. For example, 78% of the women who arrived on the Mayflower died the first winter. Natives did not provide jobs, hospitals, schools, colleges, roads, food stamps, etc. It was dangerous with homes raided and people killed, scalped and tortured by some native tribes.*

- *Third, it took many generations of sacrificing before America became a prosperous nation. The advanced technologies illegal aliens seek were not found in the New World. There was no electricity, no cars, no telephones, no computers ...*

- *Finally, our freedom came at a very high cost. Imagine the courage it took for a few colonists to take on fighting the mighty British Empire. Revolutionary soldiers were ill equipped and suffered bitter freezing cold and near starvation, yet they fought on so that they and <u>their descendents</u> could live in freedom.*

INDIA, CHINA, AND THE MIDDLE EAST

We have legal immigrants from these countries that admire our history, adopted our culture, and we are proud to call fellow citizens. However, about 40% of illegal aliens are visa violators primarily from China, India, and the Middle East that came here as guests on student, worker, or visitor visas. Their *"nation of immigrants"* excuse is baseless given the discovery of ancient mummy ancestors of Europeans in China. The Great Wall of China shows how China feels about protecting its border. India and Pakistan fight over borders. India shares a border with China yet you see little immigration comingling. How many Middle Eastern countries grant citizenship to non-Arabs?

MEXICO AND SOUTH AMERICA

America is proud to have citizens of Mexican ancestry, including some who trace back to the formation of our nation, and welcomes new legal immigrants; however, illegally crossing our borders is not ok.

"Fifty-seven Percent of Mexican Immigrants on **Welfare**," a December 2012 *examiner.com* article claimed a Center for Immigrations study found that *"nearly 50% of those immigrants originating from Mexico and Central American are here illegally."* [1033] Moreover, "Illegal Aliens Take Advantage of Tax Loophole that Costs Taxpayers Billions," a May 2012 article quoted Rep Burton who was appalled that illegal aliens were *"cheating the American taxpayer."* [1034] Mexico is *dumping its welfare cases on US taxpayers!*

Mexicans cheered when their president sent troops to protect its southern border; and illegal aliens risked prison.

Mexicans who tell Americans to go back to Europe need to look at their own European roots. Of course, Latino is from Latin. Spanish is a European Language. Antonia Lopez de Santa Anna is a European name. Conquistadors from Spain and Portugal brutally invaded and raided Latin America countries.

North American native tribes fought Mexican invaders. For example, Geronimo while hiding in a ditch heard a Mexican general tell his officers, *"Officers, yonder in those ditches is the red devil Geronimo and his hated band. This must be his last day. Ride on him from both sides of the ditches: kill men, women and children; take no prisoners; dead Indians is what we want."* [1058]

Latin America bought 17 times as many African slaves as North America. About 8.5 million slaves were shipped to the West Indies and South America, while about 0.5 million were shipped to North America. [668]

Tell Congress No Amnesty

There is a big difference when people are brought to a country as slaves and economically exploited; in contrast to people who break into a country illegally, and then economically exploit citizens. These two are not the same. They are opposite.

The illegal alien taxes billed to middle class Americans need to stop. Our government should not provide financial or other incentives to reward people for illegally entering our country. Obviously, given there are 12 to 30 million people in our country illegally, we need new INS leadership. It is time to remove rogue political leaders who try to sneak through amnesty. They are jeopardizing American lives and the future of our children. As we have learned amnesty makes illegal immigration worse.

The DREAM Act would grant amnesty to illegal aliens under the age of 35 who attend college or serve in the military. Why would we want to pay for college for illegals so they can take jobs our children need? Why would we want people who disrespected our borders in our military protecting our borders?

The 1986 amnesty rewarded the wrong people. It not only harmed the US it harmed other countries. Look at the suffering in Mexico from the drug wars. Observe how the Communist Chinese government has used outsourcing wealth to monitor and control protestors. Also, note how corruption in India has grown. We cannot afford to make this mistake again.

Chapter 16

Reclaim Democracy

"With malice toward none, with charity for all, with firmness in the right as God gives us to see the right, let us strive on to finish the work we are in, to bind up the nation's wounds, to care for him who shall have borne the battle and for his widow and his orphan, to do all which may achieve and cherish a just and lasting peace among ourselves and with all nations."
—Abraham Lincoln, March 1865

The most tragic thing about our situation is that middle class Americans reached out to help the people in China, India, and Mexico; but, our executives, our politicians, foreign executives, and foreign governments exploited our generosity. These leaders are foolish. If they destroy the American middle class, they destroy the culture that produced the wealth. They are about as smart as the people in Aesop's fable who killed the goose that laid the golden eggs.

Why did the US prosper? Clearly all nations were not equally successful. Unity, not diversity, is the secret to the US success in becoming a strong nation. Recognizing the importance of unity, our nation's forefathers named our country the **United** States, not the diversity states. Abraham Lincoln reminded Americans that a nation divided cannot stand.

Political manipulations to benefit foreign countries need to stop. Our government should answer to Americans, not to ill-gotten big money.

United We Stand–Divided We Fall

What good is it to fight Republican vs. Democrat if both parties are not representing us? Bipartisanship is only good if they are working together to benefit the American people.

How smart is it to be politically divided with management vs. labor? Both are needed to have successful companies. What we need are executives who will stop costly and destructive offshoring that leaches jobs and technology out of our country. Unions that get too big and out of control self destruct when they drain too many resources and tear down the companies essential to their survival.

It is also self destructive to be lured and divided by black vs. white politics, because our fates are intertwined.

The United States will either be united and strong; or, we will be divided and fall. We should not be fighting against each other while our government is steered off course.

We need some common sense laws that prevent executives from exploiting their positions to take unearned compensation. There should not be bonuses given when they displace US citizens with foreign workers, nor when they manipulate stock values.

We need laws that limit the size of unions so that they cannot exploit workers and companies. Employee organizations should guarantee workers are rewarded based on performance, and contributions. Employees should be treated as valuable contributors, not disposable people to be exploited and tossed aside. If Americans know they will be rewarded, not exploited then they will invent the technologies of the future. US workers should be motivated to create, to be the best in the world, to excel, and to enjoy their jobs.

Need Fair and Balanced Foreign Relations

The US needs to have a common sense approach to our foreign relations on a country by country basis. We need to adopt a good neighbor policy. Good relationships are built on mutual respect and mutual benefits.

It is time to reevaluate our impact on other countries and their cultures. We need to respect the dignity of the people from other countries. And, we must insist on honesty and integrity in our trading partners. The theft of our intellectual property is unacceptable.

Honest Jobs Reporting

Our government needs to tell Americans the truth about jobs. Job statistics reports are misleading when jobs filled by foreign visa workers and illegals are counted in the number of US jobs added. We need a law that requires companies report the number of jobs added by hiring Americans, and the number of jobs "added" by hiring foreign workers.

For example, former President Clinton claims huge numbers of jobs were created when he was President. However, the H-1B visa caps not only tripled under his administration, quota cap exemptions he signed off on for government and university jobs more than doubled the visas granted. So the quota cap may be 195,000 jobs per year, but the number of H-1Bs granted may have been 400,000. What really happened during his presidency was the mass displacement of college educated American workers by foreign workers, primarily from India. The jobs 'added' were as real as all the money most Americans made off their dotcom investments while he was president.

Warned "Budget Cuts Would Kill 70,000 Kids"

The foreign nations that are salivating over the decline of the US do not understand what they have done. They have no idea of what it took to build this nation. If the US collapses they will not be feasting on the carcass for long. Soon they will be gnawing on bones. It will be like in the movie *The Lion King*, where Scar took over the pride. There are boundaries and rules vital to prosperity. Our forefathers did not regard the Constitution as holy; but rather the Bible upon which they built the constitution as holy and the source of our prosperity.

> Recall: James Madison explained, *"We have staked the whole future of the American civilization, not upon the power of government, far from it. We have staked the future of all of our political institutions upon the capacity of mankind to self-government upon the capacity of each and all of us to govern ourselves, to control ourselves, to sustain ourselves* <u>*according to the Ten Commandments of God."*</u>

Obama's USAID Administrator, Rajiv Shah whose family immigrated to the US from India, protested proposed foreign aid budget cuts. He warned that 70,000 kids will die. That is a consequence of his native India hurting the US economy with outsourcing and offshoring. Rep. Jerry Lewis responded: *"We understand that if we don't rein in these trillion-dollar-plus deficits, programs like this one may have to be eliminated entirely in the near future."* [906]

USAID programs were started out of our nation's abundance. It is ludicrous, given our trade deficit, to borrow money from foreign nations, and then pass out the money as foreign aid. Especially, aid to nations that have harmed the US or that plot our demise.

Reclaim Control of Our Government

Americans cannot be bound by laws that were obtained by providing misinformation to Congress and/or by bribing our representatives. Foreign governments should hold no leverage over our elections. The foreign manipulation of our Government to get laws passed that harm American citizens and America must stop immediately.

The H-1B visa should be repealed. US government and technology jobs should be filled by hiring Americans. If they need training, let's train them—we have the best universities.

Politicians misdirected taxpayer money to help foreign countries and/or foreign workers compete against the US and/or US citizens. The political ring leaders behind promoting outsourcing and offshoring American jobs need to be removed. If they have endangered Americans or our soldiers they need to be prosecuted.

KNOWLEDGEABLE LOYAL AMERICAN REPRESENTATIVES

We have too many lawyers in Congress. Most of our representatives were ignorant of computer systems.

We need Americans in Congress who are knowledgeable about cyber security and understand the risks. In particular our nation needs an information security team made up of the best and brightest Americans who tried to warn Congress about how foreign students and workers jeopardized our technology leadership. Americans who lost their jobs to foreign workers should be offered jobs to advise both our government and business leaders on how to secure our computer networks.

Making & Breaking the Law

Our legal system has become a burden on our society and an instrument for exploitation. The Legal system is supposed to be about justice and about seeking the truth. It has moved far away from equal justice for all as our nation's founders intended.

From the founding of our nation our leaders recognized that for people to be free and to prosper it was necessary to have laws that protect the rights of the people, and that provide for a fair and speedy resolution of disputes.

Our justice system needs to return to its intended purpose.

In the United States, our government representatives' authority is based on the "consent of the governed." Our government is commissioned to serve us.

No representative in the US government had the right to pass laws that:

- *Caused millions of college educated US citizens to lose their jobs to foreign visa workers.*

- *Allowed stock market accounting deceptions, and subsidized executive compensation at US taxpayer expense.*

- *Taxed us to recruit and educate foreign students, and then grant visas allowing them to take jobs from US citizens.*

- *Allowed foreign outsourcing companies to set up body shops inside our nation that use foreign H-1Bs to displace American workers and to enable offshoring of high skill knowledge jobs.*

- *Increased immigration rates and granted amnesty against the will of the American people – and in some cases endangered American lives.* [63]

Picking Good Leaders?

What are the traits we need in our leaders? In his bestseller book, "Good to Great," Jim Collins' research team found that picking charismatic candidates with big egos was a bad idea. Instead, the best leaders are modest yet willful, humble yet fearless. They are good at getting the right people on board, and then putting their best people to work on the biggest opportunities. [873] George Washington fits this description.

We must also remember our President is Commander-in-Chief of the US military. Like our national emblem, we need a leader who is a peacemaker, but who is ready to fight if we must to defend our freedom. The president is entrusted with the lives of our soldiers and the very survival of our nation. It is essential that we elect a leader who they respect and trust. Our Commander-in-Chief must be all American with no divided loyalties. [873]

We need leaders who can negotiate fair trade deals with other nations that benefit the people on both sides and that do not jeopardize our culture, or our economy, or our national security.

Be Leary of "Free Trade" Candidates

Offshoring is not "free trade." Foreign nations are taking our jobs in exchange for our technology and our money. Be extra alert during the election for candidates that claim to be *"free trade"* advocates. Some promote outsourcing as if it is a pro-business stance. To the contrary, offshoring of US jobs is harmful to most US businesses. Offshoring jeopardizes patents and copyrights, trains foreign competition, harms our economy, and ultimately harms US citizens who are the main customers for most US businesses.

Reclaiming Democracy

Abe Lincoln said: *"It is true that you may fool all the people some of the time; you can even fool some of the people all the time; but you can't fool all of the people all the time."*

It is time for the sleeping giant to wake up. Not since our fight for independence has America been so burdened by foreign exploitation. The important thing you need to realize if you want to reclaim our government is that foreign nations' manipulation of our elections begins well before the primaries. Take action now. The lobbies are in DC dancing with our politicians, it's time we tapped our reps on the shoulder and break in to remind them who they are supposed to be working for. Write to your Congress members and demand reform.

We need politicians who will work for middle class Americans, not against us. Our freedom should not be for sale at any price. There are many things more valuable than money.

Do we want our candidates selected by big money? The media talks about who has enough money to stay in our political races. And where do all the millions raised for campaigning go? Much of the money goes to the media for campaign advertising. So the media has a vested interest in promoting candidates with a lot of money to spend. Maybe we ought to find a way to make it less expensive so that our candidates don't owe big favors to a few rich people. Favors we are taxed to pay for.

Where freedoms fire once burned bright, now we see black ashes. But just under that dark surface red hot coals of freedom glow red hot with passion that will reignite the fire. Deep in the hearts of passionate patriots runs the blood of our forefathers. Our forefathers put freedom above all else. Let us do the same.

Bibliography

Referenced sources are arranged in numerical order according to the reference numbers located in [brackets] in the document text. This book is the culmination of extensive research; only sources referenced in this book are included in this bibliography. Therefore, you will see breaks in the number sequence such as: reference number "6" followed by reference number "8", because reference number "7" in the complete documents list was not used in this book.

Note: Web addresses do not include the www prefix, and only contain the first part of the path. This address information or a search engine query for the title should be sufficient to help locate the articles and websites. Note also that some articles may have been removed, and some websites may have been changed from the time the research was done.

7: Jason Gabrielli, *Taking the Money: The Issue of Executive Compensation*, www.usc.edu, Web Date 5/3/2005.

8: Bruce Nussbaum, *Can You Trust Anybody Anymore?*, Business Week online, 1/28/2002.

16: Steven Weiss, *04 Elections Expected to Cost Nearly $4 Billion*, opensecrets.org, 10/21/2004.

17: *USINPAC .. Gears Up for November Elections*, usinpac.com, 10/11/2004, Web Date 11/1/2004.

18: *USINPAC .. Accomplishments*, usinpac.com, Web Date 11/1/2004.

19: *USINPAC -- Benefits to Indian American Community*, usinpac.com, Web Date 5/31/2004.

20: ITAA, *Information Technology Association of America*, www.disinfopedia.org, Web Date 10/6/2004.

22: *Highly Charged Visa Bill*, opensecrets.org, 8/3/1998, Web Date 1/30/2002.

23: Peter Schrag, *Feinstein's Rule*, prospect.org, 12/17/2001.

24: Dr. Norman Matloff, *Debunking the Myth of a Desperate Software Labor Shortage*, heather.cs.ucdavis.edu, 7/8/2001.

26: Dr. Norman Matloff, *Modern Day Slaves*, netslaves.com, 12/30/2000.

28: Rescue American Jobs, *Amazing Facts and Statistics: Non-Immigrant (Temporary) Foreign Work Visa Programs and Workers*, rescueamericanjobs.org, Web Date 5/26/2005.

30: Pradipta Bagchi, *Visas for business or bondage?*, y-axix.com, 7/6/2000.

42: Rachel Konrad, Staff Writer, *H-1B Visas Jump in 2001*, news.com.com, 1/22/2002.

52: Diane Alden, *H-1B: Bombing the Middle Class*, newsmax.com, 2/11/2003.

53: Preston Gralla, *Worker Visas Under Fire*, cio.com, 1/15/2002.

59: *Demographics of the Typical H-1B*, zazona.com, Web Date 4/24/2001.

60: *A Legislative History of H-1B and Other Immigrant Work Visas*, zazona.com, Web Date 8/11/2004.

63: Phyllis Schlafly Report, *What the Global Economy Costs Americans*, eagleforum.org, 6/3/2003.

81: Paul Craig Roberts, *Outsourcing: A Greater Threat Than Terrorism*, newsmax.com, 4/22/2005.

82: Chris Chatwood, Commentary, *A Great Sucking Sound from India*, washingtondispatch.com, 5/12/2004.

86: Chidanand Rajghatta, *US gives India Assurance on Outsourcing*, Economic Times of India, 6/14/2003.

87: Reuters, *India Software Industry Targets US Outsourcing Bill*, Reuters, 1/24/2003.

95: The Economic Times Online, *US IT Biggies Recalling BPO jobs*, economictimes.indiatimes.com, 4/28/2004.

96: Abhay Vaidya, *H-1B Cap No Big Issue for IT Firms*, economictimes.indiatimes.com, 10/31/2003.

100: David Zielenziger, Reuters, *Corrected - US Companies Quietly Moving More Jobs Overseas*, money.excite.com, 12/24/2003.

109: Bangalore, *US Firms Holding Back Offshoring Work Till Polls*, finance.indiainfo.com, 4/18/2004.

111: Mumbai Correspondent, *Outsourcing to India to rise 50% in '05*, rediff.com, 4/28/2004.

114: Technology News, *Tech Firms Defend Moving Jobs Overseas*, start.earthlink.net, 1/7/2004.

115: Manufacturing & Technology News, *Engineers Fear Offshore Outsourcing is Contributing to High Jobless Rates*, manufactuingnews.com, 11/4/2003.

120: *US Poll Results Won't Hit Outsourcing: Mulford*, rediff.com, 4/30/2004.

121: Rashmi Sharma Singh, *H Workers in Limbo*, indolink.com, 1/30/2001.

122: Terry Atlas, *Bangalore's Big Dreams*, U.S. News & World Report, 5/2/2005.

123: K.C. Krishnadas, *India's Tech Industry Defends H-1B, Outsource Roles*, Electronic Engineering Times.com, 7/10/2003.

125: United Press International, *High-tech Industry Fires Americans, Hires Indians*, newsmax.com, 3/20/2003.

127: John Ribeiro, *Study: India's Outsourcing Industry Continues to Boom*, computerworld.com, 6/3/2004.

129: Ron Schneiderman, *Outsourcing: How Safe is Your Job?*, Electronic Design, 5/10/2004.

131: Hari Sud, *US Presidential Elections 2004: Political Divide on Outsourcing*, saag.org, 1/4/2004.

138: Mike Fabrizi and Dave Michelson, *Outsourcing SWEE '98*, miter.org, 1/1/1998.

143: Rescue American Jobs, *American Jobs for Americans First - Amazing Facts*, rescueamericanjobs.org, Web Date 9/23/2003.

158: Anita Bora, *Online Outrage*, rediff.com, 6/23/2003.

173: The McAlvany Intelligence Advisor, *Red Tide: The Chinese Communist Targeting of America*, special-guests.com, 5/1/1997.

184: Mary Mosquera, *TechNet Targets Permanent R&D Tax Credit*, techweb.com, 2/24/1999.

186: Dr. Norman Matloff, *H-1B/L-1/Offshoring e-Newsletter*, engology.com, 4/4/2005.

187: Anthony Spaeth/New Delhi, *Golden Diaspora*, indianembassy.org, 3/7/2001.

195: *TechNet Members thank President Bush for his leadership in enacting a strong bi-partisan economic stimulus package*, technet.org, 3/15/2002.

213: Andrew Robinson, *Why U.S. Hands are Tied as India Readies New Missile Tests*, pacificnews.org/jinn, 1/25/1999.

222: Ted Bridis, Associated Press, *Tech Firms: We Must Export Jobs*, cbsnews.com, 1/7/2004.

223: Associated Press, *Pentagon Stands by Internet Voting System*, earthlink.net, 1/22/2004.

228: Ashank Desai, *Making of a Software Superpower*, timescomputing.com, 3/31/1999.

232: Associated Press, *India Expects Jump in High-Tech Imports*, earthlink.net, 9/30/2004.

257: Jagdish Bhagwati, *In Defense of Globalization*, Oxford University Press, 2004.

258: Biographic of Professor Jagdish Bhagwati, *Biographical Information on Professor Jagdish Bhagwati*, columbia.edu, Web Date 9/15/2005.

259: *Hegemony*, wordiq.com/definition, Web Date 8/23/2004.

260: John Pardon, IT Professionals Association of America, *The Ideological Assault on Dobbs*, itpaa.org, 10/4/2004.

266: *U.S. Political Advertising spending Reaches $1.45 billion Reports TNS Media Intelligence/CMR*, tns-mi.com, 11/1/2004.

267: Joseph Farah, *The Prince and The Media*, wnd.com, 11/7/2001.

268: Robert Morlino, *Broadcast Lobbying Tops $222 Million --One story you won't hear on the news*, publicintegrity.org, 10/28/2004.

269: Sudha Nagaraj, *US Politicians Playing with People's Insecurities*, economictimes.indiatimes.com, 4/3/2004.

270: Nancy Stellabotta, *America The Land of the Free*, cbn.com, 7/10/2003.

272: Numbers USA, *Did Congress Intend a huge Increase in Numbers after 1965?*, numbersusa.com/overpopulation, Web Date 2/27/2005.

274: Associated Press, *Foreign-Born Population Tops 34M*, Center for Immigration Studies, 11/23/2004.

275: John H. Tanton, *Commons Sense on Mass Immigration*, commonsenseonmassimmigration.us, 2/1/2004.

276: Walter F. Roche Jr. and Gary Cohn , Sun Staff, *INS Insiders Profit on Immigrant Dreams*, zazona.com, 2/20/2000.

277: Associated Press, *Bill Clinton Helps Launch Search Engine*, earthlink.net, 12/7/2004.

280: *America India Foundation -- Trustees*, aifoundation.org, Web Date 3/14/2002.

282: Lloyd Grove, *Chelsea Clinton's Start(l)ing Salary*, washingtonpost.com, 3/13/2003.

283: *Chelsea Clinton Takes a Six-figure Consulting Job*, BubbaClinton, 3/8/2003.

284: Associated Press, *Bill Clinton Backs Indian Drug Makers*, earthlink.net, 11/21/2003.

285: Paul Sperry, *Crony Capitalism, Clinton-style*, worldnetdaily.com, 2/12/2002.

286: David M Boje, *Enron is Theatre*, cbae.nmsu.edu, 9/21/2002.

287: Congressman Ron Paul, MD, *Enron: Under-Regulated or Over Subsidized?*, lewrockwell.com, 1/30/2002.

289: Melanie Warner, *The Indians of Silicon Valley*, Fortune, 5/15/2000.

322: Chindand Rajghatta, Times News Network, Washington, *Diyas Brighten White House*, indiaday.org, 10/25/2003.

323: Lesly Stahl, *Imported from India*, 60 Minutes, 3/2/2003.

325: *Where in the World is Our Colin Powell?*, hireamericancitizens.org, 3/17/2004.

333: Vanessa Richardson, *The 'Indian Mafia' Muscles onto the Web*, redherring.com, 12/14/1999.

337: Ed Frauenheim, *The Scourge of Silicon Valley –3*, salon.com, 10/19/2000.

340: Who Owns What, *Ownership of our Favorite Television Channels*, signalalpha.com, 7/7/2003.

341: Melanie Warner, Fortune, *Could Telecom be Carlyle's New Defense*, openflows.org, 3/18/2002.

342: *US Congress Heaps Praise on IITs*, in.rediff.com, 4/28/2005.

343: Shipra Arora, *Brand IIT*, dqindia.com, 6/27/2005.

356: BBC News, *India Seeks to Arrest US Scholar*, newvote.bbc.co.uk, 3/23/2004.

366: Namita Bhandare, Dew Delhi, *Indian CEOs Still Riding High in US Despite Two Exits*, hindustantimes.com, 4/12/2001.

372: AnnaLee Saxenian, *Silicon Valley's New Immigrant Entrepreneurs*, The Center for Comparative Immigration Studies, University of California, San Diego, 5/1/2000.

377: Anonymous, *I am Proud to be a Indian are You?*, geocities.com, Web Date 11/4/2002.

382: Geoffrey Barraaclough et al, *Collins Atlas of World History*, Borders Press in Association with Harper Collins, Ann Arbor, Michigan, 2003.

384: Khaleej Times Online, *Genetic Testing Reveals Awkward Truth About Xinjiang's Famous Mummies*, khaleejtimes.com, 4/19/2005.

385: Written, Produced and Directed by Howard Reid, *Mysterious Mummies of China*, PBS, 1/20/1998.

397: Philip Martin and Peter Duigan, *Recent Immigration Patterns*, Hoover Press, 2003.

401: *Williams to Introduce Foreign Aid Accountability Act*, williams2002.com, 2002.

404: *Let the Brain Drain Increase*, isa.org, 10/29/2003.

407: Richard McCormack, *Political Appointees Re-Write Commerce Department Report on Offshore Outsourcing; Original Analysis is Missing from Final Version*, manufacturingnews.com, 10/12/2005.

413: The PR Newswire, *USINPAC Organizes First-Ever India Caucus Day; Calls Upon the 143-member Caucus on India & Indian Americans to play a more effective role on behalf of community*, meadev.nic.in, 2/18/2003.

414: Rob Sanchez, *Pledge of Allegiance - To India, Part II*, The Social Contract, 2004.

417: Jim Walczak, *Free SUVs for Small Business Owners*, 4wheeldrive.about.com, 4/2/2004.

418: Lyric Wallwork Winik, *How High Can It Go?*, Parade, 10/2/2005.

424: Open Secrets, *The Big Picture: Where the Money Came From*, opensecrets.org, Web Date 11/8/2005.

425: IACPA, *Indian American Center for Political Awareness*, iacfpa.org, Web Date 11/5/2005.

426: PBS Previews 2005 (India), *The New Heroes*, pbs.org/previews/heroes/, 6/28/2005.

440: Project on Government Oversight, *Government Contractors Wield Influence Through Revolving Door, Campaign Contributions*, pogo.org, 6/29/2004.

441: The Center for Public Integrity, *The Sincerest Form of Flattery?Carlyle Group's Footsteps*, publicintegrity.org, 11/18/2004.

442: The Center for Public Integrity, *Outsourcing the Pentagon*, publicintegrity.org, 9/29/2004.

443: The Center for Public Integrity, *Outsourcing the Pentagon -- Mitre Corp*, publicintegrity.org, Web Date 12/13/2005.

444: MITRE, *MITRE About Us- Corporate Profile*, mitre.org, 1/10/2005.

446: Communications Workers of America, *Compete America! - Story of an Anti-American Worker Cartel*, cwalocal4250.org/outsourcing, Web Date 10/4/2005.

450: Sandra J. Boyd, Chair Compete America, *Compete America - The Alliance for a Competitive Workforce*, competeamerica.org/hill/letter congress, 10/3/2005.

457: Roosevelt, *Theodore Roosevelt on Immigration*, posted blog, 12/29/2005.

459: Plyler v. Doe, *U.S. Supreme Court: Plyler v. Doe*, tourolaw.edu/patch/Plyler/, 6/1/1982.

468: Gary Cohn and Walter Fl. Roche, Baltimore Sun, *Indentured Servants for High-Tech Trade Labor*, ailf.org/pubed/n022100a.htm, 2/21/2000.

484: Michael Fitzgerald, *Is U.S. Losing the Innovation Arms Race*, cioinsight.com, 6/5/2005.

485: *Innovation Takes More Than Just Ambition*, cioinsight.com, 6/5/2005.

486: Council on Competitiveness, *2003 Competitiveness and Security Survey*, 1500 K Street, NW, Suite 850, Washington, DC 200005, 202-682-4292., 12/1/2003.

487: Council on Competitiveness, *Innovation Partners*, innovateamerica.org/partners/partners default.asp, Web Date 2/10/2006.

514: Scott Baldauf, *India History Spat Hits US*, abcnews.go.com/International, 1/1/2006, Web Date 3/2/2006.

521: India Express - India Mumbai, *USINPAC Indian Toehold in US Political Whirlpool*, usinpac.com/NewsContent, 11/19/2002.

523: multiple authors, *Technology Without Borders Global iit2005 Conference*, iit2005.org, 2005.

524: Jagdish Bhagwati, *Muddled and Maddening*, Wall Street Journal, 9/13/2004.

525: Sridhar Krishnaswami, *Expert Assails Kerry's Trade Policy*, The Hindu Business Line, 9/14/2004.

543: Mike Clendenin, *EEs Fatalistic About Design Offshoring*, Electronic Engineering Times, 8/7/2006.

544: George Leopold, David Roman, *Quashed Report Tracks Design Exodus*, Electronic Engineering Times, 7/31/2006.

553: Michael D. Lemonick, *Are We Losing Our Edge?*, Time, 2/13/2006.

556: SourceWatch, *Information Technology Association of America from SourceWatch*, sourcewatch.org, Web Date 2/18/2006.

558: *TechNet: Who We Are, Meetings with US Politicians, and Members,* technet.org, Web Date 3/22/2006.

559: Mother Jones, *John Doerr (with Ann), Donor Profile,* matherjones.com, 3/5/2001.

560: NNDB Tracking the Entire World, *John Doerr,* nndb.com/people, Web Date 3/23/2006.

571: Nicholas Haschka, MIT, *Kicking the SUV Fix,* thetriplehelix.org, 8/18/2005.

575: Matt Kelly, Associated Press, *Iraq: 10 US Contractors Penalized,* corpwatch.org, 4/26/2004.

581: Associated Press, International Herald Tribune, *Doctors strike at Indian Hospitals to Protest Affirmative Action,* iht.com, 5/14/2006.

593: PakNews, *Enron's India Connections Likely to Haunt Clinton,* paknews.com, 2/22/2002.

601: Wikipedia, *N.R. Narayana Murthy,* wikipedia.org/wiki, Web Date 4/15/2006.

605: U.S. Citizenship and Immigration Services, *Citizenship,* uscis.gov, Web Date 3/23/2006.

610: People's Daily Online, *Indian Police Arrest 11 Hindus,* english.people.com.cn, 5/29/2002.

614: Associate Press, *Cherokee Bar Salves' Descendants,* , 3/4/2007.

615: Ron Schneiderman, Contributing Editor, *Offshoring. Outsourcing. Out of Work.,* Electronic Design, 10/20/2005.

618: Wikipedia, *Non-Resident Indian and Person of Indian Origin,* en.wikipedia.org/wiki/Non-resident Indian and Person of Indian Origin, Web Date 3/9/2007.

625: US India Political Action Committee, *USINPAC,* http://www.usinpac.com, Web Date 4/9/2007.

637: Terence P. Jeffery, *In Government, Too? You'll Find Illegal Aliens in the Darndest Places,* the-two-malcontents.com, 6/25/2007.

638: Anne E. Kornblut, *Obama Apologizes for Punjab-gate,* washingtonpost.com, 6/19/2007.

642: Kristin Collins, Staff Writer, *Foreign Workers Balk Over Backlogs, They Protest Years' Wait for Green Card*, newsobserver.com/news, 11/11/2007.

647: Lisa Zagaroli, McClatchy Newspapers, *Bundling' of Campaign Funds Masks Large Donations: Growth in 'uber-fundraisers' May Result from Restrictions in Other Aspects of Campaign Financing*, accountability-central.com, 11/19/2007.

656: T. Christian Miller, Times Staff Writer, *Private Contractors Outnumber U.S. Troops in Iraq*, latimes.com/news/nationworld/world, 7/4/2007.

657: *$2.2 Trillion Illegal Alien Taxpayer Sticker Shock*, worldnetdaily.com/news, 4/11/2007.

660: *Washington's Farewell Address*, wikisource.org/wiki/Washington's_Farewell_Address, 1797.

664: Critics of the Act, *Immigration Reform and Control Act of 1986*, wikipedia.org/wiki/Immigration_Reform_and_Control_Act_of 1986, Web Date 1/7/2008.

667: Franklin D. Roosevelt, *Franklin D. Roosevelt D-Day Prayer*, historyplace.com/speeches/fdr-prayer.htm, 6/6/1944.

668: Hugh Thomas, *The Slave Trade: The Story of the Atlantic Slave Trade: 1440-1870*, Touchstone Rockafeller Center, New York, New York, Copyright 1977.

672: Emily Bazar, USA Today, *Immigrants Sue to Speed Citizenship Applications*, usatoday.com/news/nation/2008, 2/21/2008.

675: Jay MacDonald, *Hummer Tax Break Gets Hammered*, bankrate.com/brm/itax/biz, 1/20/2005, Web Date 2/11/2008.

676: Associated Press, *U.S. Stretches Hours to Help Immigrants Become Citizens*, usatoday.com/news/washington, 3/22/2008, Web Date 3/22/2008.

677: Client Alert, *AILA Exploring Contact Congress Find Your Officials*, capwiz.com/aila2/home/, Web Date 3/22/2008.

692: *Woman, Baby Die After Doctors Refuse to treat Them in India*, foxnews.com, 4/25/2008.

694: Haya El Nasser and Paul Overberg, *Census: Fewer Young Workers to Support U.S. Growth*, usatoday.com, 5/1/2008.

697: *Bobby Jindal*, en.wikipedia.org, Web Date 5/14/2008.

698: *A McCain Huckabee Ticket? The Right Reacts*, usnews.com/blogs/, 5/13/2008.

701: Henry Chu, Los Angeles Times, *As India's Wealth Rises, A Woman's Limited Dowry Could Mean Her Death*, epilot2.hamptonroads.com/Respository, 9/23/2007.

702: *World Population Balance*, worldpopulationbalance.org, Web Date 12/24/2007.

705: Associated Press, *High School Wartime Sets Soldiers' Kids Apart*, att.net/scripts/editorial, Web Date 5/23/2008.

706: Paul Elias, Associated Press, *Veterans Affairs Official Denies Cover-up of Suicide Rates*, foxnews.com, 4/25/2008.

710: Frontline/World, *Jesus in China*, pbs.org/fronline world, Web Date 7/24/2008.

713: *Oath of Citizenship (United States)*, en.wikipedia.org, Web Date 2/3/2009.

714: *Demographics of United States 1990 -2001*, en.wikipedia.org, Web Date 12/3/2008.

716: andhra-pradesh-news, *Hyderabad Police Arrest 25 Foreign Students for Overstaying*, newkerala.com, 10/22/2008.

717: Sujeet Kumar, *Police Probe Assault on 50 "Witches"*, reuters.com, 12/22/2008.

721: Manjeet Kripalani in Bombay, *Private Equity Pours Into India*, businessweek.com, 6/20/2005.

723: Stephanie Armour, USA Today, *2008 Foreclosure Filing Set Record*, usatoday.com, 1/14/2009.

736: William Baue, *War Millionaires; Defense Contractor CEO Pay Up 200 Percent Since 9/11*, socialfunds.com, 9/1/2005.

748: India Today on the Net, *50 Power People*, indiatoday.com, 2/21/2005.

749: SAJAforum, *Diwali: White House Celebrates Diwali*, sajaforum.org, 10/14/2009.

751: Morley Safer, *60 Minutes Profiles Bobby Jindal*, sajaforum.org, 3/1/2009.

781: Rhys Blakely in Bombay, *Hindu Extremists' Reward to Kill Christians, as Britian Refuses to Bar Members*, timesonline.co.uk, 11/20/2008.

782: Rahaf Harfoush, *Yes We Did, An Inside Look at how Social Meida Built the Obama Brand*, New Riders Voices that Matter, Copyright 2009.

783: Bob Hepburn, *New Faces Join Community Board*, thestar.com, 9/30/2006.

784: Associated Press, *In Key States, Latino Vote fueled Obama's Victory*, nydailynews.com, 11/20/2008.

785: US Department of State, *Syria*, state/gov, 2/28/2005.

786: Barack Hussein Obama, *I will be a President who Draws Upon the Energy and Expertise of the Indian-American Community*, India Abroad, 2/29/2008.

787: Corey Dade, *In Criticizing Cleanup, Jindal Finds His Voice*, online.wsj.com, 6/2/2010.

788: RaviKhanna, Washington, *Indian PM Becomes President Obama's First State Guest*, voanews.com, 11/22/2009.

789: Alec MacGillis, *Obama Administration Plans to Close International Labor Comparisons Office*, washingtonpost.com, 3/3/2010.

790: IndiaPost - Voice of Indians Worldwide, *Obama Tax Plan to Hit India IT*, indiapiost.com, 8/5/2009.

794: Jake Tapper and Matthew Jaffe, *Will GM Spend Taxpayer Bailout Money on Overseas Operations?*, abcnews.com, 11/16/2009.

795: Fredreka Schouten, USA Today, *Top Obama Fundraisers Get Posts*, usatoday.com, 10/28/2009.

796: Associated Press, *Poll: Trust in Big government Near Historic Low*, foxnews.com, 4/19/2010.

797: Sunita Sohrabji, India West, *Obama Names Indian Americans to Key Legal Posts*, newamericamedia.org, 1/23/2009.

798: Galen Gruman, InfoWorld, *Meet the Nation's First CIO*, cio.com, 3/6/2009.

799: Bill Warner, *Barack Obama and Slavery*, americanthinker.com, 9/26/2008.

800: McCainPalin 2008, *Fill Critical Shortages of Skilled Workers to Remain Competitive*, johnmccain.com, 10/24/2008.

801: Ephriam Schwartz, *Clinton, McCain and Obama on H-1B Visas*, infoworld.com, 2/26/2008.

802: Erika Lovley, *Report: 237 Millionaires in Congress*, dyn.politico.com, 11/6/2009.

803: Douglas Magmann and Judi McLeod, *Media Blackout on Obama Eligibility Dates Back to November*, canadafreepress.com, 8/4/2009.

804: Aaron Klein, WND, *White House Boasts: We 'Control' News Media, Communications chief offers shocking confession to foreign govenmrnt.*, wnd.com, 10/18/2009.

805: Viji Sundaram, India-West Staff Reported, *Obama Campaign Stiffs Ethnic Newspaper*, New America Meida, Expanding the News Lens through Ethnic Media, 8/25/2008.

806: Eric Sshawn, Fox News, *Charges Against 'New Black Panthers' Dropped by Obama Justice Dept*, foxnews.com, 5/29/2009.

807: Grant McCool, *Obama fund-raiser faces new US fraud allegation*, reuters.com, 9/2/2009.

809: Chelsea Schilling, WorldNetDaily, *Obama Justice Department Shut Down ACORN Probe, FBI docuemtns 'relfect systematic voter registration fraud'*, wnd.com, 3/12/2010.

810: The Steady Drip, *Obama: More evidence for election fraud charges*, thesteadydrip.blogspot.com, 11/2/2009.

811: DPA, *Obama Raised Record $745 Million in Presidential Campaign*, twocircles.net, Web Date 12/7/2008.

812: Kenneth R. timmerman, *Secret, Foreign Money Floods Into Obama Campaign*, newmax.com, 9/29/2008.

813: Pamela Geller, *Obama's Foreign Donors: The Meida Averts Its Eyes*, americanthinker.com, 8/14/2008.

815: Carla Marinucci, Chronicle Political Writer, *Obama Reaps Big Bucks at S.F. Fundraisers*, sfgate.com, 8/18/2008.

816: Wikipendia, *Vivek Kundra*, en.wikipedia.org, Web Date 3/9/2009.

817: The Times of Inda, *India-born Executives Leading Candidates for Obama Tech Job*, timesofindia.indiatimes.com, 1/17/2009.

818: Kim Zetter, *Phantom Obama Vote Appears on NJ Voting Machine*, blog.wired.com, 4/30/2008.

819: SAJAforum, *Resources for 2008 Presidential Race: The 2008 U.S. Presidential Race & South Asians / South Asia*, sajaforum.org, Web Date 10/21/2008.

820: SAJAforum, *Obama Apologizes for Campaign 'Screw-up'*, sajaforum.org, 6/18/2007.

822: SAJAforum, *Obama Digs in, Plays the Outsourcing Card*, sajaforum.org, 6/15/2007.

823: SAJAforum, *Iowa-Obama's South Asian Support*, sajaforum.org, 1/4/2008.

824: SAJAforum, *The Top Indian-American Bundlers*, sajaforum.org, 1/11/2008.

826: SAJAforum, *Hillary's Indian Supporters Move to Obama*, sajaforum.org, 6/18/2008.

827: SAJAforum, *Survey: Likely Indian Voters Overwhelmingly Support Obama (Q&A)*, sajaforum.org, 10/19/2008.

829: Reverend Jonas Clarke, *No king, but King Jesus*, timetracts.com, 12:00:00 AM.

830: SAJAforum, *Prez Race: U.S. Election Day Events in India*, sajaforum.org, 11/2/2008.

831: SAJAforum, *2008 Electon" South Asians Voted Overwhelmingly for Obama*, sajaforum.org, 5/18/2009.

833: SAJAforum, *Prez Race: Obama Tells South Asian Audience, "I am Desi" and Talks About6 Abilityto Make Dal*, sajaforum.org, 8/19/2008.

834: Susan Page, *The Biggest Political Winners and Losers of 2009*, usatoday.com, 12/12/2009.

835: NDTV Correspondent, New Delhi, *Mike Huckabee: Profile*, ndtv.com, 7/11/2008.

836: Matthew Lee and Julie Pace, Associated Press, *White House Names Foreign Aid Chief*, goggle.com, 11/10/2009.

837: SAJAforum, *Prez Race: Indians Plan to Gift Obama with a Gloden Hanuman*, sajaforum.org, 6/23/2008.

838: Ishani Duttagupta, ET Bureau, *Indian Americans Very Visible at Democratic National Convention, The Economic Times*, economictimes.indiatimes.com, 9/4/2008.

839: William Lajeunesse and Fox News, *Lobbyists Enjoy Windfall Despite Pledges to Rein in Special Interest Influence*, foxnews.com, 4/1/2010.

840: Associated Press, *Bill Clinton's Foreign Affairs May Cost Clinton Chance of Secretary of State*, elections.foxnews.com, 11/15/2008.

841: SAJAforum, *Prez Race: Mike Huckabee's Promise to Amend the Constitution*, sajaforum.org, 1/29/2008.

842: Netlore Archive, *U.S. Miliatry Deaths Since 1980, Racial Demographics*, urbanlegends.about.com, Web Date 11/16/2008.

843: Martha T. Moore ad Paul Overberg, USA Today, *Gap Between Baby Boomers, Young Minorities Grows*, usatoday.com, 5/14/2009.

844: Frank James, NPR's News Blog, *Campaign Money From Foreign firms May Be Coming*, npr.org/blogs, 1/22/2010.

845: danfmarsh, *Fourteenth Amendment Debate*, numbersusa.com/overpopulation, 12/7/2007.

846: WND, *New U.S. tourism: Anchor Babies Aweigh!*, wnd.com, 3/22/2010.

847: Aaron Klein, WND, *Obama Adviser: Amnesty to Ensure 'Progressive' Rule*, wnd.com, 2/2/2010.

848: Bob Unruh, WND, *Electoral College Scam: Where Dead People Vote*, worldnetdaily.com, 12/2/2008.

849: Discussion with Alan Binder, Jagdish Baghwati, Sherrod Brown?, *Future of Trade in the Global Economy*, Charlie Rose Show, 5/5/2009.

850: Ed Barnes, Fox News, *Illegal Immigration Costs U.S. $113 Billion a Year, Study Finds*, foxnews.com, 7/6/2010.

852: The Mac Observer, Time Article - Prince's Statement, *Saudi Prince Al Waleed Goes Spending Again*, macobserver.com, 11/1/1997.

853: ThinkProgress.org, Center for Media and Democracy, *Saudi Prince, Now Part Owner of Murdoch's News Corp, Influences Fox News,* prwatch.org, 2/10/2010.

854: Danile Tencer, Raw Story, *Murdoch, Saudi Prince Team Up to Lauch 'Arabic Fox News',* sott.net, 7/9/2010.

855: Dana Blanton, *Fox News Poll: Most OK With No Protestants on Supreme Court,* foxnews.com, 4/28/2010.

857: Associated Press, *Financial Overhaul Provision to Promote Diversity Hiring in Federal Agencies Stirs Backlash,* foxnews.com, 7/10/2010.

858: Associated Press, *Dem Lawmakers to Call for Suspension of Stimulus Going to Foreign Firms,* foxnews.com, 3/3/2010.

859: Associated Press, *Panel: Gov't Bailout of AIG Was 'Poisonous',* foxnews.com, 6/10/2010.

860: Michael Snyder, *The Middle Class in America is Radically Shrinking. Here Are the Stats to Prove it,* theeconomiccollapseblog.com, 7/15/2010.

862: Aaron Klein, WND, *Obama Advisor: U.S. 'ideal place of renewal of Islam',* wnd.com, 7/20/2010.

865: Bill O'Reilly and John Stossel, *Is University of Minnesota Planning to Teach 'White Guilt' Class?,* foxnews.com, 12/16/2010.

866: Class Notes, *Resources for Teaching About White Privilege,* ctlupdates.wordpress.com, Web Date 8/25/2010.

867: Comments by Dr. Alan Berman and others, *Suicide Rates of Teenagers: Are Their Lives Harder to Live?,* query.nytimes.com, Web Date 11/16/2008.

868: *CBO: Eight Years of Iraq War Cost Less Than Stimulus Act,* foxnews.com, 8/30/2010.

869: Associated Press, *Saudi Government, Other Nations Donate Millions to Clinton Foundation,* foxnews.com, 1/1/2010.

870: Associated Press, *State Department Waste in Iraq Costs Billions, Audit Finds,* foxnews.com, 1/25/2010.

871: Associated Press, *U.S. to Double Civilian Force in Iraq After Withdrawl,* foxnews.com, 8/19/2010.

872: Bill O'Reilly, *Who's Looking Out for You?*, Broadway Books, New York, Copyright 2003.

873: Jim Collins, *Good to Great*, HarperCollins Publishiers Inc., 10 East 53 rd Street, New York, NY, 10022, Copyright 2001.

874: The Washington Times, LLC, *ICE Agents Vote 'No Confidence' in Leaders, Say Amnesty Coming*, newsmax.com, 8/9/2010.

875: cchmelenski, *Sen. Durbin to Bring Dream Act Amnesty to Senate Floor*, numbersusa.com, 9/22/2010.

877: Matthew Mosk, Washington Post Staff Writer, *Obama Accepting Untracable Donations*, washingtonpost.com, 10/29/2008.

878: Edwin Mora, *Rupert Murdoch Calls for Amnesty for 'Law-Abiding' Illegal Immigrants*, cnsnews.com, 9/30/2010.

880: Ed Barnes, Fox News, *Citizens' Group Helps Uncover Alleged Rampant Voter Fraud in Houston*, foxnews.com, 9/25/2010.

881: Posted by Catalina Camia, *Two Ex-Senators Join Major Lobbying Firm*, usatoday.com, 1/11/2011.

882: Maxim Loft, *Immigrant Who Voted Illegally on Road to Becoming a U.S. Citizen*, foxnews.com, 8/26/2010.

883: *18 Former ACORN workers Have Been convicted or Admitted Guilt in Election Fraud*, foxnews.com, 11/26/2010.

884: John Azumah, *The Legacy of Arab-Islam in Africa*, Oneworld Publications, 12/25/2001.

885: Cathering Dodge, *Obama Excitement Wanes as Young Voters Tune Out U.S. Election*, bloomberg.com, 10/25/2010.

886: Percy Fernandex, *Dual Citizenship" NRIs Should Pay Tax Too*, Times of India, 7/29/2005.

887: IANS, *Indias Holding Dual Citizenship Must have Tax Obligations in India*, thaindian.com, 1/8/2010.

888: Roh Hira, Ph.D and Anil Hira, *Outsourcing America:The True Cost of Shipping Jobs Overseas and What Can be Done About It*, AMACOM, a division of American ManagementAssociation, New York, NY, Copyright 2008.

890: Bradley Keoun and Craig Torres, *Foreign Banks Tapped Fed's Lifeline Most as Bernanke Kept Borrowers Secret*, bloomberg.com, 4/1/2011.

891: Eric Shawn, *A Family of Minnesota Man with Mental Disabilities Says He is a Victim of Voter Fraud*, foxnews.com, 4/5/2011.

892: Debbie Siegelbaum, *GOP says 5,000 non-citizens Voting in Colorado a 'wake-up call' for States*, thehill.com, 3/31/2011.

893: Aaron Klein, WND, *Obama Religion Adviser Linked to Unindicted Co-conspirator*, wnd.com, 7/26/2010.

894: William Lajeunesse and Fox News, *Taxpayer Calculator: How Much Will the Transition to Digital Medical Records Cost You?*, foxnews.com, 9/2/2010.

895: Ed Barnes, Fox News, *Up to $1 Billion in U.S. Aid Winds Up In Taliban Coffers*, foxnews.com, 10/22/2010.

897: James White, *$200m-a-day' cost of Barack Obama's Trip to India will be Picked up by U.S. Taxpayers*, dailymail.co.uk/news, 11/2/2010.

898: TNN, *Obama Acknowledges Decline of US Dominance*, timesofindia.indiatimes.com, 11/8/2010.

899: Ed Barnes, Fox News, *Internet Voting Arrives? But is it Secret and Safe?*, foxnews.com, 11/1/2010.

900: Shannon Bream, *Justice at the Justice Department?*, foxnews.com, 9/30/2010.

901: Pauline Jelink, The Associated Press, *Report: Too Many Whites, Men Leading Military*, navytimes.com, 3/7/2011.

902: *Meet the New Americans*, pbs.org/independentlens/newamericans, Web Date 3/30/2004.

903: *Birthing Centers for Chinese Women Looking to Have American Babies Uncovered in California*, foxnews.com, 3/25/2011.

904: Vijay Prashad, *Now, the Real Test for Bobby Jindal*, hindu.com, 11/16/2007.

905: Emily Wax, Washington Post Foreign Service, *Christians Face Hindus' Wrath*, washingtonpost.com, 9/15/2008.

906: Stephen Clark, Fox News, *Obama Official: GOP Budget Would Kill 70,000 Kids*, foxnews.com, 4/1/2011.

907: Jonathan Tilove, The Times-Picayune, *Gov. Bobby Jindal Releases His Birth Certificate*, blog.nola.com/politics, 5/6/2011.

908: Dan Gainor, *Why Don't We Hear About Soros' Ties to Over 30 Major News Organizations*, foxnews.com, 5/11/2011.

909: James H. Walsh, *George Soros: Open Society Open Borders*, newsmax.com, 7/25/2006.

910: George Soros, *The Age of Fallibility: Consequences of the War on Terror*, PublicAffairs, New York, NY, Copyright 2006.

912: Miriam Jordan, *Immigrants Benefit as Economy Recovers*, The Wall Street Journal, wsj.com, 10/30/2010.

913: yogmama, *Naked Body Scanner Manufacturer's CEO Obama's Guest on Trip to India*, Daily Paul Liberty Forum, 11/22/2010.

914: The Editors, *Eerie Echo' of Mortgage Crisis in Student Loan Debt*, thechoice.blogs.nytimes.com, 5/31/2010.

915: Henry Unger, *Student Loan Debt is Now More than Credit Card Debt*, The Biz Beat, 4/12/2011.

916: Anand Giridharadas, *A College Education Without Job Prospects*, nytimes.com, 11/29/2006.

917: Chi-chu Tschang, *China's College Graduate Glut*, chinaeconomicreview.com, 6/5/2007.

919: Jennifer Epstein, *Sharron's Angle" Harry Stole election*, politico.com, 6/10/2011.

920: Associated Press, *Banks Repossess 1 Milliion Homes in 2010*, foxnews.com, 1/13/2011.

921: Tony Munroe and Peter Henderson, *India's IT Aims to Soften Image as Obama Visits*, reuters.com, 10/27/2010.

922: USINPAC, *USINPAC Member Details*, usinpac.com/trackCongress, Web Date 7/13/2011.

925: Linda Ong, *DREAM Act Immigration Activists*, asianweek.com, 8/7/2010.

931: Audrey Hudson, *Illegal Aliens Step Boldly Out of the Shadows at DREAM Hearing*, humanevents.com, 6/30/2011.

932: George Soros, *The Capitalist Threat*, Atlantic Monthly, Volume 279, No. 2, 2/1/1977.

933: David Horowitz, and Richard Poe, *The Shadow Party: How George Soros, Hilary Clinton, and Sixties Radicals Seized Control of the Democratic Party*, Nelson Current, Nashville, TN, Copyright 2006.

934: Maxim Loft, *Billinaire George Soros Trying to Stack the Couts, Critics Say*, foxnews.com, 6/27/2011.

935: Chuck Neubauer, *Soros and Liberal Groups Seeking Top Election Posts in Battleground States*, washingtontimes.com, 6/23/2011.

936: *Guide to the George Soros Network*, discoverthenetworks.org, Web Date 7/22/2011.

938: *Weiner's Mother-in-Law a Member of Muslim Brotherhood*, wnd.com, 6/18/2011.

939: *US-India Nuke Deal Wins Support from Key Congressman*, indianmuslims.info, Web Date 7/13/2011.

940: Kimberly Dvorak, *Dvorak: Immigration Think Tank Sees Birthright Citizenship as Threat to US Security*, federalobserver.com, 3/15/2011.

943: Matthew Cardinale, *First Federal Reserve Audit Reveals Trillions in Secret Bailouts*, globalresearch.ca, 8/29/2011.

944: NDTV Profit, New Delhi, India, *President Obama's Team India*, YouTube, 9/7/2010.

973: *AeA, ITAA Announce Merger*, techamerica.org, 12/9/2008.

974: Project Vote Smart, *HR 3012- Repeals Certain Green Card Limitations*, votesmart.org, 1/5/2012.

976: Sarah Ryley, *The Daily Exclusive: Rubber Stamp*, thedaily.com, 1/3/2012.

979: NDTV, *Long Wait for Green Cards Could Soon Be Over*, ndtv.com, 1/7/2012.

981: *Benefits of Green Card*, immihelp.com, Web Date 1/6/2012.

984: Mahwish Khan posted, *"A Republican Probably Can't Win Without About 40 Percent, Minimum, of the Hispanic and Latino Vote"*, americasvoice.com, 1/6/2012.

991: cchmeielenski, *Recent College Grads Suffering in Job Market as Pres. Obama Asks for More Foreign Workers in their Fields*, numbersusa.com, 5/19/2011.

993: *Indian-Americans: Candidates Supported by USINPAC*, usinpac.com/candidates-supported.html, Web Date 1/16/2012.

994: Center for Immigration Studies, *Three Decades of Mass Immigration: The Legacy of the 1965 Immigration Act*, cis.org/articles/1995, 9/1/1995.

995: Dylan Stableford, *Time Magazine Apologizes for Putting non-Latino on 'Yo Decido' Cover*, news.yahoo.com, 2/24/2012.

1024: Doug Powers, *Obama to See India on $200 Million a Day*, michellemalkin.com, 11/2/2010.

1025: Max Fisher, *Poll Finds 20 of 21 Countries Strongly Prefer Obama*, washingtonpost.com, 10/23/2012.

1026: *Media as the "Fourth Estate"*, usfaca.edu/fac-staff/boaz, 2/2/2012.

1027: Becket Adams, *Business Soros Warns of 'Riots,' 'Brutal' Clampdowns & Possible Total Economic Collapse*, theblaze.com, 1/24/2012.

1028: Matthew Vadum, *George Soros Funds Occupy Wall Street*, humanevents.com, 10/21/2011.

1029: beckj, NumbersUSA, *Media Mum on Amnesty for Illegal Aliens Who Commit Idntity Felonies*, numbersusa.com, 9/25/2012.

1030: Perry Chiaramonte, *96 Percent of Ivy League Professors' Donations Went to Obama*, foxnews.com, 11/28/2012.

1031: Oliver Darcy, *University Sponsors Campaign to Undermine 'White Privilege'*, d-umn.campusreorm.org, 6/20/2012.

1032: Terence P. Jeffery, *Obama Increased Foreign Aid 80%; Spent 76% More on Foreign Aid Than Border Security*, cnsnews.com, 10/2/2012.

1033: Bob Wilson, *Fifty-Seven Percent of Mexican Immigrants on Welfare*, examiner.com, 12/1/2012.

1034: Hannah Miller, *Illegal Aliens Take Advantage of Tax Loophole that Costs Taxpayers Billions*, numbersusa.com, 5/1/2012.

1037: Adam Popesu, *Foreign Workers in the US Send Billions Home*, marketplace.org, 6/3/2011.

1038: Stefan Wagstyl, *Remittances Set to Grow Even Faster than Expected*, Financial Times, 11/21/2012.

1039: Associated Press, *1.9 Million 2011 Foreclosures are Fewest Since 2007*, usatoday.com, 1/12/2012.

1040: Tyler Durden, *Uncle Sam Books 50% Loss As government Motors Buys Back 200MM Shares from Tim Geithner*, zerohedge.com, 12/19/2012.

1041: Taylor Rose, *Family Chain Migration to Flood US*, wnd.com, 12/17/2012.

1043: Annie Groer, *Indian-Americans Gaining Clout in US Politics*, politicsdaily.com, 10/24/2010.

1044: Van Esser, *Over 50,000 Illegal Aliens Received Amnesty, Work Permits under Obama's DACA Program*, numbersusa.com, 11/19/2012.

1045: Kathy Shaidle, *Did Illegal Aliens Steal the Election for Obama?*, wnd.com, 11/23/2012.

1046: WND, *The Big List of Vote Fraud Reports*, wnd.com, 11/13/2012.

1047: American Dream, *22 Signs That Voter Fraud is Wildly Out of Control and The Election was a Sham*, rightsidenews.com, 11/16/2012.

1049: Kenric Ward, *VA: Military Absentee Ballots Going AWOL in 2012*, watchdog.org Virginia Bureau, 9/6/2012.

1050: Shane McGonigal, *Campaign Donations from University Employees Went Overwhelmingly to Obama*, campusreform.org, 11/14/2012.

1052: Shaila Dewan and Mark Landler, *Drop in Jobless Figure Gives Jolt to Race for President*, nytimes.com, 10/5/2012.

1053: Crowley, *Town Hall 2012 Presiential Debate*, 10/16/2012.

1054: Roy Beck, *Obama Speech Brags About 3 Million New Jobs (Fails to Mention 3 Million New Foreign Work Permits)*, numbersusa.com, 1/24/2012.

1055: Jessica Vaughan, Center for Immigration Studies, *Mayorkas to USCIS Staff: Just Say Yes-Or Else!*, cis.org, 10/1/2010.

1056: Gregg Zoroya, *Troops' Families Feel Weigh of War*, usatoday.com, 8/4/2009.

1057: OpenSecrets.org, *Industry Long-Term Contribution Trends*, opensecrets.org, 12/26/2012.

1058: *Geronimo's Mightiest Battle*, firstpeople.us, Web Date 12/27/2012.

1059: Senate Republican Conference, John Thune, Chairman, *The Obama Economy Isn't Working*, republican.senate.gov, 9/17/2012.

1060: Dave Eberhart, *Soros: Obama, Romney 'Not Much Difference'*, newsmax.com, 1/28/2012.

1061: Terence P. Jeffery, *4 Yrs at Private College = $130,468; Median-Priced Existing Home =$173,100; US Debt Per American Under 18 = $215,676*, cnsnews.com, 11/4/2012.

1062: Lois Romano, *Obama's Data Advantage*, politico.com, 6/9/2012.

1063: Craig Timberg and Amy Gardner, *Democrats Push to Redeploy Obama's Voter Database*, washingtonpost.com, 11/20/2012.

1067: Elvina Nawaguna, Reuters, *Student Loan Write-Offs Hit $3 Billion in First Two Months of Year*, chicagotribune.com, 3/25/2013.

1068: Conor Freidersdorf, *President Obama's DREAM Act Executive Order*, theatlantic.com, 9/1/2013.

Index

How to Take Back Our Jobs and Build a Bright Future.

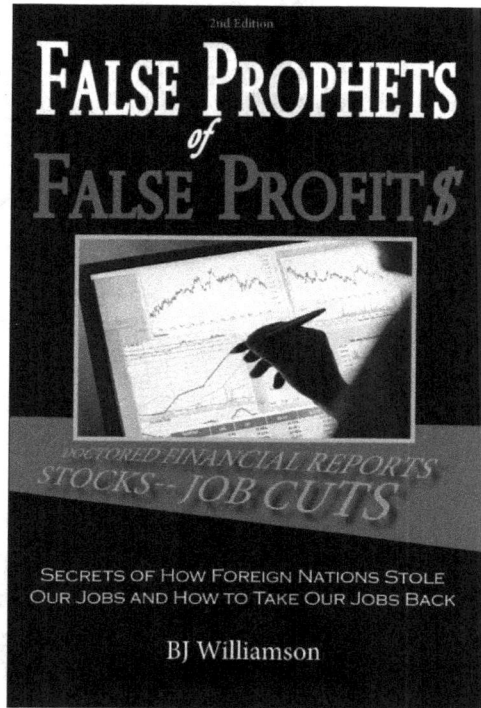

Learn the hidden secrets behind job losses to foreign workers, and how foreign investments manipulated our stock market. You will find many surprises, and most importantly an economic model that shows how we can restore our economic prosperity.

To Order <u>False Prophets of False Profits</u>

go to: <u>*Amazon.com*</u>

Or to learn more go to: <u>*www.lanitepublishing.com*</u>

What We Need to Do to Protect Our Economic Competitiveness and National Security.

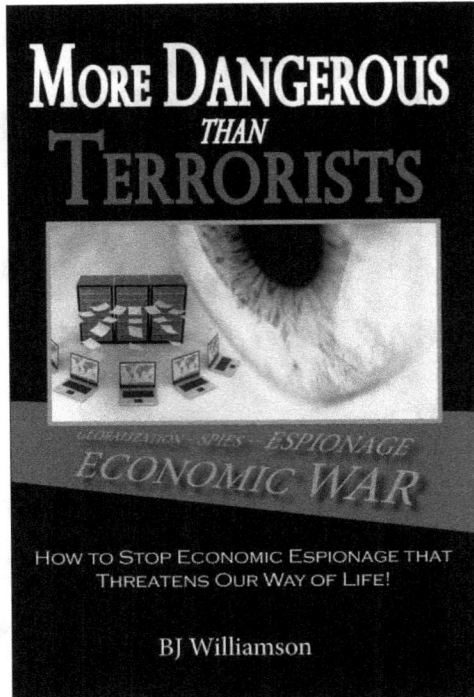

www.ingramcontent.com/pod-product-compliance
Lightning Source LLC
Chambersburg PA
CBHW060852280326
41934CB00007B/1014